Raptured

The Final Daze of the Late, Great Planet Earth

Earl Lee

See Sharp Press, LLC • Tucson, Arizona

For information contact

See Sharp Press, LLC
P.O. Box 1731
Tucson, AZ 85702-1731

www.seesharppress.com

Lee, Earl, 1954–
Raptured : the final daze of the late, great planet earth / by Earl Lee – Tucson, Ariz.: See Sharp Press, 2007.
192 p. ; 23 cm. – (Kiss my left behind ; 1)
ISBN 1884365426 (pbk.)

1. End of the world – Fiction. 2. Rapture (Christian eschatology) – Fiction. 3. Illinois – Fiction. 4. Parodies. 5. Fantastic fiction. 6. Christian fiction.
813.54

Printed in Canada

ONE

Captain Ramrod Steel leaned back in his pilot seat and closed his eyes. He tried hard to imagine what the slim, blonde flight attendant would look like wearing his pilot's cap and not much else.

Captain Ramrod Steel was tall, dark and ruggedly handsome—a real man's man. He had been watching this young, blonde flight attendant for several weeks. Over the past few days he had carefully tested the waters: flirting a bit here, smiling a bit there, a firm pat on her tight little butt every so often.

Ramrod figured out from her nameplate that she was "Hadshe D."and he thought Hadshe was the hottest little flight attendant this side of a Los Angeles AA meeting. Yes, Hadshe was a real stunner, and Ramrod spent a lot of his free time trying to imagine what this young and perky honey blonde might look like under her tightly stretched flight attendant's uniform.

Not that Ramrod's "Little Missus"—his wife Ireme—wasn't an attractive woman. Mrs. Ramrod Steel was still very pretty, in a housewifely sort of way. Ireme was 5'8" and, despite having two kids, she was still a perfect 36-24-36. But Ireme had her flaws. She was, unfortunately, a natural brunette—and yet Ramrod had fallen in love with her, and he had even married her, in spite of this major personal failing. Somehow Ramrod found love in his heart for Ireme, even though she wasn't a blonde. Yet, it was like life had dealt him a pretty good hand, except for that Two of Clubs. And it still bothered him. During their twenty years of marriage, Ramrod often told himself that life was not always fair, much less honey blonde.

But even though Ramrod often flirted a bit with the female flight attendants, he was still strongly attracted to his wife Ireme. It was their love life that was the real problem. Weekly service was simply not enough to satisfy Ramrod physically. He tried to blame the whole problem on their religious differences, and particularly his wife's obsession with her new church. Ireme spent a lot of time doing volunteer work at the church. And when she became a "born again" Christian, she insisted on intimate relations only on Wednesday morning, just before she went to church. Ramrod, on the other hand, wanted it at least six days a week—and on the seventh, well, Ramrod would happily volunteer to service Ireme on Sunday morning, before church began—and he would gladly promise not to block the aisles while doing it.

Not that Ramrod wasn't religious. He had no real quarrel with religion, in moderation, and he often went to church on Sunday with Ireme and their two kids. Ramrod was very proud of his older daughter, Cloye, even if she was a girl. Cloye was a coed, who was now away at Bible college. Ramrod loved her, even though she took after her mother, and especially after her mother's stubborn streak.

And then there was Doray—their only son. He was a real momma's boy. Doray's unnatural attachment to his mother bothered Ramrod a lot. His son was just not manly enough. He had failed at sports. Even T-ball was too rough and physical. Worse yet, young Doray didn't seem to be much interested in girls, not even the pretty, blonde cheerleader sort of girls who went to the new church. Not even that new girl Sarah, the sixteen-year-old blonde with the big smile and the perfect D-cup breasts.

Ramrod was mildly interested in his wife's new church. He even tossed an Abe Lincoln in the collection plate every once in a while. It was God who was the real problem. What really bothered Ramrod about God was that he—Ramrod—always felt he was in competition with Him.

"Does Ireme love God more than she loves me?" Ramrod would say to himself while looking in the bathroom mirror.

Worse yet, when he and Ireme were having wild passionate marital relations, Ireme often called out "Oh God! Oh God!" not "Oh Ramrod! Oh Ramrod!" And this bothered Ramrod a lot. It was like God was getting all the credit for *his*—Ramrod's—performance.

"Why does everything have to be about God?" Ramrod groused, while Ireme was humming the hymn, "Onward Christian Soldiers." It didn't help that Ireme often prayed to God afterwards, thanking Him for Ramrod's enormous endowment.

Ramrod tried to be a good husband. Except for "sinning in his heart" he was faithful to Ireme, even on his overnight flights to

Europe. But Ramrod's imagination did commit all sorts of sin. Ramrod's many fantasies were filled with nonstop sinning. His mind tended to wander over all the possibilities that might lie ahead of him with various flight attendants, and especially the young and nubile Ms. Hadshe D.

At the same time Ramrod was haunted by the weird sermon preached last Sunday and the way Reverend Bobby Black kept looking over at him and nodding. It was a kind of double nod—the same kind you saw in bars when two studdly guys are recognizing each other as "players." At first Ramrod was worried, because he thought Reverend Black might be coming on to him. But as he thought about it, Ramrod realized that Reverend Black was trying to convey a message, or signal him, . . . or something.

Just last Sunday Reverend Black had preached a sermon on The Rapture, and he made it sound like this sermon should be extra-extra important to Ramrod—like his eternal soul depended on understanding what would happen in The Last Days. But Ramrod didn't understand the whole "End Times" theology.

After the sermon, as they walked out of the church, Ramrod asked Ireme what she thought about the sermon and the strange way Reverend Black was acting during the service. As usual, Ireme quoted a couple of Bible verses that Ramrod didn't understand, and then she walked away smiling a beatific and annoyingly self-righteous smile.

It was like Fate had a message for Ramrod. Later that same afternoon, while sitting on the sofa and waiting for the football game to start, Ramrod watched a religious documentary on one of the PBS channels. In this program, an "End Times" expert named Dr. Harold Cox talked about the coming Tribulation.

Dr. Cox was introduced as "America's foremost expert on Revelations and The End Times." His new TV program was the first of a series of religious documentaries that Dr. Cox produced for the local Public Broadcasting station. This program was part of a new "religious education" emphasis at PBS. Much of the cost of producing the program was underwritten by grants from the National Endowment for the Humanities and the Department of Education. Dr. Cox's popular companion textbook, *Ready for The Rapture?* was also heavily promoted by the federal No Child Left Behind Program.

Dr. Cox was a solid-looking elderly gentleman. Actually he

looked a bit like former President Ronald Reagan, and Dr. Cox played on this resemblance. He even imitated Reagan's little head-bobbin' movement and wore the same hair cream favored by the ex-President. Dr. Cox began the program by describing how, at the beginning of The Great Tribulation, thousands of believing Christians would simply disappear. One minute a Christian would be standing next to you, talking to you, and the next minute he would vanish—called to Heaven by God. This was called "The Rapture."

Even more distressing, Dr. Cox described the unbelievable chaos that would happen at The Rapture, as thousands of believing Christians, who might at that moment be driving automobiles or operating heavy machinery, would suddenly vanish. Their now driverless autos would careen madly all over the highways, killing or injuring nonbelievers. The TV program even included a graphic simulation of cars crashing and airplanes flying into buildings.

That was several days ago, and this idea still bothered Ramrod. He worried about what would happen if he suddenly disappeared from the cockpit of his 747 as it flew thousands of feet above the Atlantic on its way to O'Hare airport. How many people would die if this 747 suddenly nose dived into the ocean?

Ramrod leaned forward in his seat and flicked on the autopilot.

"No point taking chances," he thought. Maybe the co-pilot, Jesus Ramirez, could land the huge 747 alone. "But what if he's a Christian, too?" It was unlikely that anyone else on board could safely land the big 747—it was just too complex a piece of machinery. "Well," he thought, "if that's God's plan, to let them crash into the ocean and die a terrifying death, their bodies torn to pieces in the impact, then who am I to interfere?"

Ramrod leaned back in his seat and stared at the pint carton of chocolate milk that Hadshe had brought him earlier. There was a picture on the carton of a teenage boy, not much older than his own son Doray, and the slogan "Have you seen this child?"

This idea rolled around in Ramrod's mind for a while, mainly because there was little else occupying it, and Ramrod began to get concerned. "What would happen if Ireme, Cloye and Doray suddenly disappeared, called to Heaven by God?" This disturbing idea existed in Ramrod's head for about five seconds.

Then he thought, "Hey, I haven't seen Hadshe for at least fifteen minutes." The idea that the wife and kiddies had been called to God didn't bother Ramrod nearly as much as the idea that the delectable Ms. Hadshe might now be out of reach, called to Heaven along with the rest.

Leaving the autopilot in place, Ramrod made his way back to the passenger compartment, hoping to find Hadshe serving drinks in First Class, or even fluffing pillows in Coach. It didn't make any sense, but he had to make sure she was still here.

It was dark, the sky on the horizon behind them just beginning to fade into the cover of night. Most of the passengers were asleep, but Ramrod noticed a lot of empty seats—more than you'd usually find on these night flights from London. Ramrod began to worry again.

"Where the hell is Hadshe?" he thought.

He searched through the galley, went through the passenger area a second time—still no sign of Hadshe. "Maybe she's already been taken up to Heaven," he thought. Then, just ahead, he saw the forward bathroom door. He tried it.

The door was not locked, in fact it was slightly ajar; so Ramrod pulled on the door to reveal . . . Hadshe in the toilet with the co-pilot!

"What's going on here!" Ramrod said.

"Oh . . . well he's just had a small problem with some milk spilled on his pants," Hadshe said as she slowly turned around.

Ramrod looked down and saw a small wet stain slowly spreading itself on the copilot's dark blue trousers. The copilot had a startled, deer-caught-in-the-headlights expression on his face. Meanwhile, Hadshe was holding a tissue and smiling innocently at Ramrod.

"OK, I was just wondering where you were," Ramrod said as he turned and walked away from the guilty-looking pair. A glimmer of suspicion raised its ugly head in Ramrod's otherwise unoccupied mind. "Why did she take him in the toilet to clean his pants? She could have done that easier in the galley, or even in the cockpit." Becoming annoyed, Ramrod returned to the cockpit.

On the way he noticed an old woman. She was sitting there next to an empty seat—empty except for a jacket, a pair of glasses, and a pair of shoes. "Maybe the old guy just wandered off without his shoes and stuff," Ramrod thought. But then he became worried again. It was just like the "End Times" expert, Dr. Cox, had said. People would simply vanish, leaving behind their clothes . . . or at least most of their clothes. "After all," Ramrod thought, "you'd still need pants in Heaven, at least for modesty's sake."

As Ramrod mulled this over, he realized when his wife's religious compulsions had first begun. A few years ago, Ireme had stopped attending the Catholic Church. Instead she started going to a small church where people were encouraged to speak in tongues and wave their arms in the air, as if they were human lightning rods for the God Juice cumming down from the sky. Then Ireme got involved in supporting "God friendly" businesses. Ireme became an Amway distributor and quietly encouraged Doray to work as a delivery boy for Domino's Pizza.

It wasn't difficult to find businesses that were obviously "God friendly," as all she had to do was look for advertisements that featured a Christian "fish" symbol. Ireme believed in putting her checkbook behind her beliefs. She donated heavily to Focus on the Family and to the 700 Club, not to mention the dozens of other Christian charities that quickly identified her and added her name to their mailing lists.

Even with the good money her husband made as a pilot, it was difficult for Ireme to manage her household funds when so much money had to be sent out to various charities. Ireme began to cut back on some of the family's more frivolous expenses, and she applied for four or five new credit cards to make it easier to manage. Occasionally she had to cut back on the 10% that she regularly tithed to the local congregation, but she tried to make up the difference by volunteering her time to all the church-sponsored events.

Soon Ireme was spending a lot of time Sunday afternoons picketing in front of local "gay friendly" churches, carrying her handmade sign: "God hates Faggs." Then she found herself picketing every Wednesday afternoon in front of the Womyn's Health Clinic. Ireme knew that they didn't actually perform abortions there, but she suspected that they wanted to. Not only that, but they gave out birth control information and even gave out condoms to teenagers. The last straw came when she found out that they gave out free needles to drug addicts as part of their anti-AIDS program. She remembered her minister shouting through his bullhorn: "AIDS is God's punishment on fags and drug addicts!" Ireme had nodded her head, agreeing that these clinic workers were interfering with God's judgment on those perverse, inhuman monsters.

One day Ramrod tried to confront his wife over her extravagant donations to various religious charities. Ireme had responded sweetly, simply saying that it was important to do "God's work." Ramrod said, "Why doesn't God do his own work! Why does God need *you* to do his work for him?"

Ireme smiled blissfully and said, "Someday you'll understand." Then she went back to writing out checks to the Bibles for Prisons program, the Bibles for Arabs program, and an extra large check to the Bibles for Israel program.

* * *

While Ramrod was making his way back to the cockpit, a young TV reporter named Mark Doody was working away frantically on his laptop. Mark was slightly built and had a high-pitched voice. He resembled the actor Jason Lee, or maybe the teenage Corey Haim, or maybe even Jennifer Jason Lee—except that Mark was less masculine looking. His name was Mark, but some people called him "Bark" because he strongly resembled a small terrier in the way he interviewed people. His high voice was like a constant "Yap! Yap! Yap!" as he questioned people on camera about their left-wing biases, their lack of patriotism, or—worse yet—their ingratitude toward the President for making America strong again.

Privately, most reporters thought of Mark as "the next Geraldo" or—given his pre-pubescent appearance—"the next Carlson Tucker." And many wondered, given his vivid imagination and his lack of regard for the facts, why he didn't already have his own show on a cable news channel like Fox or MSNBC. Certainly Mark's right-wing biases were as exaggerated as his opinion of his own abilities. Like Lim Rushbaugh, Mark had realized, early on in his career, that loud-mouthed "media personalities" got paid a lot more than reporters who tried to be unbiased.

But it was as a war correspondent that Mark really made his reputation. During the Iraq War, he spent three weeks embedded with the swabs on the USN aircraft carrier Abraham Lincoln. Afterwards, Mark hinted to his co-workers that he should get the nickname "Buck" because that's what the sailors called him. And so this was the nickname that stuck.

There were, however, some dissenters. One of his co-workers suggested that Mark should be called "Hoss." Given his small stature, this nickname seemed a bit odd; but in terms of his willingness to believe almost any bullshit story that came along, Mark did resemble the character "Hoss" on the old western TV series Bonanza.

Mark believed that he led a charmed life. He frequently got the best assignments and the best opportunities to interview famous people. Mark thought he was lucky, but his co-workers thought—given his limited abilities—that some supernatural power had to be involved. Some even speculated aloud that Mark had sold his soul to Satan—and gotten a pretty good deal. Few people suspected the truth: Mark's career was being guided from above by powerful men who had their own plans for Mark's future.

That morning Mark was on his way to interview the man who was likely to become the next head of the United Nations. This man was an Eastern European warlord named Nickelay Dubyah. Mark was already on a first-name basis with the dictator, and Mark wanted a story about Dubyah's newfound relationship with the Israeli government.

Mark had fallen onto this story by accident. No one else knew about Nickelay's secret deal with the Israelis. Mark only learned about the deal while interviewing a famous Nobel Prize-winning Israeli scientist.

Mark had come back from Israel a few weeks earlier after interviewing the famous chemist, Dr. Chumm Rosegarden. Rosegarden was a heavyset man with a florid complexion and an addiction to video games. Because of several snowboarding accidents, skateboarding accidents, and a series of car accidents while playing Gran Turismo, Dr. Rosegarden was confined to a wheelchair—at least several hours a day. With his newly purchased "Go-Go Super X Ultra Travel" electric wheelchair (with the inboard potty), he could now give inspirational tours of his top secret facility on an hourly basis. Between tours he was usually found playing his Playstation, which was mounted in a wire basket between the steering handles.

During the interview with Mark, the elderly Dr. Rosegarden had led him out to his secret laboratory, a bunker-style block building which sat in the middle of a field. It was here, on the edge of the Israeli desert, that Rosegarden was raising corn, beets and even pumpkins!

Dr. Rosegarden explained, while demonstrating the liquid recycler attachment of his new wheelchair, that simple irrigation had failed to improve the land. Instead it was necessary to develop a new fertilizer that could turn this sandy, barren desert into a veritable Garden of Eden.

"And what is the secret of this new fertilizer?" Mark asked.

"I have developed a process to turn recycled government paper into a particularly rich fertilizer. It doesn't work with ordinary recycled paper, but government paper seems to convert into an especially rich manure-like substance. Just look at that corn!"

Mark saw the field of corn with its magnificent ears, some a foot long or more. Dr. Rosegarden had achieved similar results with cucumbers, beans, tomatoes, even radishes. With this single discovery, Dr. Rosegarden had developed a fertilizer that could eliminate world hunger.

In the months since his discovery, the state of Israel had turned this wasteland into a magnificent garden. The process could do the same in other countries, particularly in countries with an abundance of waste paper. The state of Russia was particularly interested in getting its hands on the formula, given that they had little hard currency and many tons of worthless government papers left over from the old Soviet empire, not to mention the Yeltsin era.

In fact many governments around the world were interested in the formula, including the United States, although the American government was not particularly interested in the new fertilizer, except for export. They were more interested in having a justification for destroying many millions of pages of government paper, some of which could be "inconvenient" if they ever came to light.

Of course the worst culprit was The Pentagon, which handed out lucrative government contracts, worth billions, to friendly corporations without a bid process. There were literally hundreds of thousands of documents pointing to a culture of corruption and political favoritism in Washington. And the discovery of this new fertilizer, which could only be made with government paper—well, many in the current administration called it a "God send."

Even with the cooperation of the well-heeled Washington Press Corps, there was always the danger that some small media outlet might get its hands on these papers and expose the corruption in Washington. Eventually the stink would rise so high that even the major New York media outlets couldn't ignore it.

But Dr. Rosegarden refused to sell the formula.

Instead the Israeli government was importing thousands of tons of paper and converting it into fertilizer. There was enough fertilizer to enrich the desert lands of all Israel's neighbors. But there was no way that Israel could process enough paper to satisfy all the governments outside the Middle East.

Many governments wanted the formula, especially the Russians. After failing to get their hands on the formula, the Russians decided to attack Israel and take the formula by force. And, by pure accident, the Russians planned their attack to begin at dusk that very night.

That evening, as the day faded into dark, Dr. Rosegarden took Mark on a tour of his lab. For some reason, which was never fully explained, Dr. Rosegarden's laboratory also served as the central command for the Israeli Ministry of Defense. And so, when the Russian bombers, fighters, and missiles were launched at Israel, Mark Doody was there, camera in hand, to record the event—assuming, of course, he wasn't squished like a cockroach in the terrible onslaught.

Luckily the Russians decided not to use their nuclear weapons, since they wanted to grab the secret formula, not disintegrate it.

As the Russian bombers, fighters and missiles approached the borders of Israel, sirens rang out and people ran quickly to the nearest bomb shelter. The Israeli air force was caught off guard. Besides, it was too late to launch a realistic defense against the many thousands of missiles and planes now headed toward them.

And then the miracle happened: Russian airplanes collided with Russian missiles; fighters went off course and slammed into bombers. In a matter of minutes the skies over Israel were filled with explosions from thousands of aircraft and missiles knocked accidentally from the overly congested sky.

Luckily for Israel, the Russians had relied on their cutting edge Serbo-Slavic technology in building the guidance systems for their weapons. The result was that most of the missiles either fell short, landing on Syria and Turkey, or they overshot the mark and landed in Egypt. One missile went so completely off course that it landed in the Vatican and launched several cardinals and a dozen altar boys into the next world.

The missiles that didn't go off course, instead collided with Russian aircraft. In a matter of several minutes virtually every missile, bomber and fighter was destroyed. Realizing the extent of the disaster, the Russians quickly decided to hightail it back to friendlier territory. Israel won the war without firing a shot.

Mark Doody crawled out of his hiding place and managed to film the last few seconds of explosions in the sky above. Dr. Rosegarden yelped "Zelda!" ("Happiness" in the ancient Hebrew dialect) and then declared, "It's a good thing they attack us on the holy day of Ros Hashish or our soldiers would really have give them a whipping!"

Some of Mark's friends saw his narrow escape from death as The Hand of God working in Mark's life. But Mark was still uncertain about what all this meant. Mark considered himself to be a confirmed skeptic, a paragon of Unbelief. Even years ago when he was in high school, working part time on *The St. Louis Singles News*, Mark wrote in his "credo":

"I'm a Skeptic. And I'm a Journalist. I look up things in the library—a lot! I believe in the motto of Missouri, the 'Show-me, don't just blow me' state. I need evidence. I need demonstrations. I need show and tell. Even though I pray to God every once in a while, especially when I'm in trouble—which for most guys my age is every 28 days—I still think deeply about the issues and don't automatically jump to a religious or mystical answer to questions. I am, by nature, doubtful about the existence of God, and even whether He is a He or a Her. I don't believe in New Age stuff. For me, 'Past Life Regression' means not calling a girl after she gives me her phone number. Sure I own a lucky rabbit's foot, a lucky penny, a lucky 4-leaf clover and a lucky horeshoe [sic], and a pair of lucky underwear and several pairs of lucky socks that I only wash every seven days. But under it all I am a died-in-the-wool skeptic."

TWO

Captain Ramrod Steel sat quietly in his pilot's seat, staring at the blue sky over the Atlantic, or at least what you could see of the sky above the heavy white clouds. He leaned back and tried to rest his eyes for a minute. It was hard to stay alert during these long transatlantic flights, and Ramrod fought to stay awake. Even though he wanted to avoid these thoughts, his mind kept wandering back to the lusciously delightful Hadshe. Finding her in a compromising position with the co-pilot merely added a new edge to Ramrod's desires. He tried to imagine what she was doing at that moment. He closed his eyes and thought of Ms. D. bent lusciously over a cart full of soft drinks and snacks. The delightful way Hadshe's skirt pulled up, rising above the seam of her calf-length boots, filled Ramrod with a burning passion. Ramrod could not resist this opening. He came up behind her, put his huge hands on her expansive backside and then pressed up against her, forcing his enormous . . .

Suddenly Chris, the token "gay" flight attendant, burst in and flung himself against Ramrod's body. His expression was terrified, as he forced his face into Ramrod's manly chest, crying, "They're gone! They're gone!"

At first Ramrod was embarrassed by the emotional outburst. Chris was pressing against Ramrod's partly aroused manhood, and Chris didn't seem to care about how this bothered Ramrod. Then Ramrod became annoyed. The last time this happened, Chris had gone off the emotional deep end because he had discovered that all the condoms were missing from the cockpit's emergency medical kit. Ramrod had tried to explain that the medical kit never had condoms, but Chris was too distraught to listen. Finally Chris had cried out, "But what if we crash on a desert island! We have to have condoms!" But this time something was different. Chris had a look on his face that combined horror, and fear, and even more horror. "They're gone!" he croaked, through his tear-stained, flesh-toned Clearasil. "They . . . are . . . all . . . gone!"

Obviously this time it wasn't just a matter of missing condoms, or not having enough warm nuts. This time it was serious.

Ramrod grabbed Chris by the shoulders and bellowed, "Who's gone?"

Suddenly Hadshe looked through the curtain and said, "Captain Steel, most of the passengers are gone!"

Steel moved to the curtain and looked out. It was true. Dozens of seats were empty.

But where could they be?

Captain Steel decided to look for them.

He looked here, he looked there,

He looked up, he looked down, he looked all around,

No one in the galley, no one in the toilet, no one in the cockpit.

They were just plain gone.

About half the passengers were missing.

Suddenly Ramrod remembered Dr. Cox's lesson about The Rapture.

"Two men are standing in a field, one will disappear. Two women will be washing clothes, one will vanish. They will be called to Heaven by God."

Ramrod's head swam with ideas. It had happened. The End of the World.

The flight crew looked to Ramrod for leadership. But he didn't know what to do next. Then he had an idea.

"Get me the passenger list."

Minutes later Captain Steel was walking up and down the corridors, trying to figure out if there was some kind of pattern to the disappearances. Sitting in front of him were a priest and a nun. "Still here" he muttered to himself. Then he looked at the occupations of people who were now missing: a pipefitter, a gardener, a truck driver, a nurse, a plumber, a housewife, a librarian, a doctor. Also missing were a professor of Business Ethics, a Colonel of Military Intelligence, and the President of the American Association for Corporate Responsibility.

They were gone, but there was no clear pattern.

Then Ramrod began to look at who was "left behind": a marketing executive, a philosophy professor, a salesman of non-cling baptismal gowns, an evangelist, the CEO of an electric utility, the inventor of a new type of cell phone, a mid-level executive for a chain of nursing homes, a lawyer who represented HMOs, an FBI agent, a dozen or so mid-level federal bureaucrats, two federal judges, an SEC investigator, the director of a mutual fund, five insurance executives, four music executives, three recently graduated MBAs, two school administrators, a priest, and a nun.

Why were some taken and others "Left Behind"?

It just didn't make sense.

* * *

Mark Doody leaned forward in his seat. The old woman sitting in the seat just in front of him was poking him with her finger.

"What is it?" Mark said.

"He's gone."

"Who's gone?"

"My husband. He's disappeared."

Mark leaned forward and twisted his head around. Yep, the seat was empty.

"Where did he go?" Mark said.

"I don't know . . . and he's left his clothes behind."

Mark stood, pulling himself up out of his seat, and looked down at the cushion that had, until recently, held Fred Muertz, a retired construction worker. Mrs. Muertz had a desperate look on her face.

"Could you look for him?" she said.

Mark climbed over the passenger next to him, slipped on his penny loafers and began walking up and down the aisle.

It was early morning, and Mark wasn't used to getting up before noon. He went along the aisles, looking for Fred and a toilet, and especially the toilet, as his bladder was overactive from all the cola and warm nuts he had sucked down. Just then Mark saw the flight attendant Chris pushing through the aisles, coming toward him.

"I'm looking for someone," Mark announced.

"Aren't we all," Chris responded, then pushed past Mark on his way toward the back of the aircraft.

Mark went to the toilet, then returned to his seat.

Mrs. Muertz had a hopeful expression on her face as he approached.

"No sign of him," Mark said. "Maybe he's busy joining the mile-high club."

As he climbed back into his seat, Mark bumped the guy next to him. Mark quickly said, "Did you see what happened to the passenger sitting in front of you?"

"The old guy? No I didn't."

Mark sat back and pulled the blanket over himself. Suddenly he couldn't remember if he had washed his hands or not after using the toilet. Then he noticed that the seat across from him was empty, too.

* * *

Ramrod Steel made his way through the plane, trying to comfort the young women who—like himself—were left behind. The co-pilot was trying to radio for instructions, but there was no response and they were far out over the Atlantic. In another hour they would be within sight of the East Coast, but until then they were on their own.

Some of the passengers were becoming hysterical. Ramrod grabbed one woman and shook her, then slapped her hard across the face. She started crying and collapsed into a vacant seat, crushing the suit coat, shirt and pants on the empty seat under her into a wrinkled mess.

Ramrod returned to the cockpit and got on the intercom system. He tried to explain The Rapture and how it signaled the beginning of The Great Tribulation. He tried to describe The End Times. But none of it made much sense to the passengers. All they knew was that some people were taken to Heaven by God; the rest were left behind to be punished under the iron fist of The Antichrist. People began to panic.

A group of business executives broke into the booze cart and began gulping down its tiny bottles of liquor. Others had already raided the galley and come out with dozens of cans of beer and bags of pretzels and chips. Several college-age students broke into their supplies of wacky weed, and a young man who was smuggling a brick of hashish in his backpack also contributed to the growing intoxication.

It was as if, suddenly, the world had changed and all the old rules were gone. The disappearance of all these people—in mid-air no less—meant that all the rules of physics were wrong, all the ideas of science gave way to a belief in magic and the powers of The Invisible. Even gravity was a question mark. In spite of the fact that the 747 glided over the Atlantic, proving the reality of aerodynamics, none of the passengers on board knew enough about science to be able to distinguish this from magic. If people could disappear in mid-flight, then everything was possible and nothing was impossible. Magic, spells, prayers, curses—suddenly every form of mystical belief became possible, even probable. In a matter of minutes, people who had been brought up on the 18th-century pragmatic values of Ben Franklin were seized with the wild-eyed mysticism of Reverend Cotton Mather, the Puritan witch-hunter.

People were either saved or damned. That was it. And so The Damned, who were now left behind, decided to have a party.

As they got closer to the Eastern seaboard, Captain Steel was able to pick up radio broadcasts. The world was engulfed in chaos.

Listening to the cockpit radio, Ramrod could hear the reports of terrible fires, floods, earthquakes, massive car crashes and traffic pileups. In New York a volcano had opened up in the middle of Wall Street, in Philadelphia a gigantic bolt of lightning shattered the Liberty Bell, in Trenton a black man drove his new Porsche across town without being pulled over by the cops. All manner of bizarre and miraculous events took place, and all were breathtaking in scope. In North Carolina the heads of all eight major tobacco companies promised to pay the health care costs of lung cancer victims—out of their own pockets! A TV evangelist in Virginia admitted that all of his faith healings had been faked. A politician in Washington DC actually voted his conscience and sponsored a single-payer health care system. Even more amazing, the Chair of the SEC promised to crack down on corporate crime—and meant it!

All these strange and miraculous events were reported by radio broadcasts that reached the inbound 747. Ramrod didn't know what to do. Even if they landed safely in Chicago, they would still face a world gone mad—or at least very, very weird.

Ramrod got up out of his seat and left the cockpit, making his way back to the passenger compartment. In first class he saw a group of businessmen drinking and dancing. They had all pulled off their jackets and ties, except for those who wore their ties like headbands. Several flight attendants had joined the party, and a conga train was forming. They were doing shots as they went past the galley. A professional stripper had come up from coach to entertain them. Ramrod realized that the social fabric of the 747 was coming unraveled, or at least unglued.

Ramrod pushed on past the first class and went through the curtain into the coach area. There the scene was even more bizarre. A group of college students had lit up a bong and were passing it around. Another group—mostly college students—were stripping off their clothes. They piled their clothes on top of the clothes of those who had "disappeared." A nun was on her knees on the floor, where she was counting her rosary beads, mumbling under her breath. Meanwhile, the priest was chasing a young boy around the cabin. At one point the priest almost had the boy cornered, his gray, claw-like fingers snatching at the boy's clothes.

Then it happened.

Suddenly a bunch of devils appeared, out of thin air. Ramrod decided that they were devils because (A) they had red skin, except for the "yellow devils" who had yellow skin, (B) they had tiny sets of horns, and (C) they had long tails that came to a sharp arrow-like point.

One of the devils grabbed the small boy, tearing him from the priest's lecherous grasp, and then disappeared. Other devils grabbed the rest of the small children and carried them off, just like the winged monkeys carried off Toto in The Wizard of Oz.

Ramrod suddenly remembered Reverend Black's teachings about Original Sin. In his view (and the commonly accepted view of biblical scholars going back to the Middle Ages), all humans are born with Original Sin, because of Eve eating The Apple in the Garden of Eden. Because of Original Sin, all humanity is doomed, damned to suffer in the pit of Hell. For this reason, all unbaptized children are destined for Hell. So it only made sense to Ramrod that, just as some people would be carried off to Heaven, others were doomed to be snatched by devils and taken to Hell. Even unborn babies are doomed to suffer in Hell forever.

At that moment a man opened the door of the toilet, and a whole bunch of devils came running out, like clowns emptying out of a tiny circus car. One of these devils, dressed like a circus strongman, came waddling out of the toilet. He was carrying a gigantic mallet. A second devil pushed a pregnant woman to the floor and pinned her there. Then a third devil suddenly appeared, wearing an enormous catcher's mitt.

The "strongman"devil spit on his hands, grabbed the handle of the mallet and swung it over his head like he was planning to ring the bell at a carnival. This devil slammed the mallet down on the woman's belly, and an unborn baby shot out of her stomach, just like strawberry jelly being squirted out of a jellyroll. The third devil caught the baby in his catcher's mitt and then disappeared with the baby, carrying it off to its new home in Hell.

The rest of the passengers were horrified. Some ran to other parts of the 747, trying to escape. Soon every child and unborn baby on the airplane had been carried away by devils.

Ramrod was too shocked for words. He wandered back to the cockpit and sat down. His whole world was coming apart. But here, sitting in the pilot's seat, there was some sense of familiarity which helped him hold it together.

At that moment Hadshe entered the cockpit, came up behind him, and placed her hands on Ramrod's massive shoulders. Her blue nails dug into his flesh and brought a wince to his face. “Hadshe . . .” he said.

Before he could say more, Hadshe leaned over him and planted her mouth on his. Her nimble tongue was already working its way through his words, so that all he could utter was a garbled “nggh, goohh, aaagguuu.”

Hadshe took his words to mean “I love you, marry me, ride my face like a Harley!”—though not necessarily in that order.

For a fraction of a second the thought of his wife and kids passed accross Ramrod’s mind, like the flash of varicose veins on a Vegas showgirl. But, luckily for Hadshe, there was nothing to obstruct this thought as it went through.

Hadshe broke off the passionate kiss long enough to climb on top of Ramrod and press his face into her ample bosom.

“Oh, Ramrod,” she said, “there’s nothing left out there for us. Nothing we can depend on. All that we have is our love for each other.”

Ramrod’s response was a muffled, “nggh, goohh, aaagguuu.”

As if in a vision, Ramrod saw Hadshe standing in his kitchen at home, wearing nothing except an apron. And sitting at her feet was their infant son, little Ramrod Junior, who was clearly—even at this young age—very masculine looking. The little tyke even had the shadow of a moustache on his upper lip. It was like a personal vision of paradise.

“Thank you, God!” Ramrod exclaimed.

And then the vision dissolved.

Suddenly he felt a hand on his arm.

“You okay Buddy?”

Ramrod opened his eyes. He looked over and saw Jesus sitting there. The co-pilot had a concerned look on his face.

Hadshe evaporated into his dreams. The cockpit was empty, except for Ramrod and his co-pilot, and they were rapidly descending toward Chicago's O’Hare airport.

Ramrod leaned forward in his seat, his mouth filled with a sick, cottony taste. “Chicago,” he said, “. . . oh, crap!”

* * *

Hadshe Dunhim thought about her future. During the flight she paid particular attention to a young TV correspondent traveling in coach. She recognized him from his news reports and realized quickly that Mark Doody could help her move up in the world. It took her only seven minutes to convince Mark to put in a word for her with the Dictator Nickelay Dubyah, who was soon to be the most powerful man in Eastern Europe.

Nickelay Dubyah was the son of Nickelay the Elder, formerly Fearless Leader, Dictator and Supreme Commander of the Former Soviet Republic of Texrectumstan. Nickelay the Elder was widely known as "The Butcher of Baghdad" for the way he brutally invaded the country of Iraq and tried to assassinate his former friend and ally, Sodom Hussein.

Dubyah the Younger had to work to overcome the hard feelings left behind by the brutal rule of his vicious and overbearing father. In college, young Dubyah struggled to overcome the disadvantages of Wealth and Power, not to mention an addiction to Cold Turkey body shots, cocaine and blondes. But now his time had finally come. A secret deal with the Nobel prize winning scientist Dr. Chumm Rosegarden was about to make Dubyah the Younger the most powerful man in the world.

And powerful men need beautiful women. Especially honey blondes.

THREE

The huge 747 was directed to park near the O'Hare international terminal, but it was not allowed to connect to the mobile walkway because of mysterious "personnel problems." All the moving stairs were already in use, so the passengers were forced to disembark by sliding down the big plastic emergency chutes.

Hadshe Dunhim escorted the young journalist, Mark Doody, to the door of the plane. Her long robin-egg blue nails were planted firmly in the flesh of his soft bicep.

"You're with the *Weekly Whirled News* now aren't you?" she said to Mark as she pointed him toward the open door.

"Yes, yes I am," Mark said, as he clutched his laptop to the concave smoothness of his chest.

Hadshe slipped her business card into his pants pocket, letting her nimble fingers hesitate there for a few seconds.

"I bet you've never had a woman's hand in your pants before," she murmured in his ear, "at least not to put something *in*."

Mark blushed red as Hadshe shoved him onto the evacuation chute and he tumbled end over end, finally landing in a crumpled pile on the tarmac.

"That'll leave a mark," she said, tossing a large carry-on bag onto the plastic chute after him.

* * *

As her father's 747 was landing at O'Hare, Cloye Steel was driving her old Buick LeSabre along Highway 55. She was heading home, toward Chicago.

Cloye had been expelled from college.

It all started six months ago. Cloye had gotten into an argument with her mother Ireme about whether kissing was really sex or not. Ireme strongly believed that any physical contact between two people was in some way "sexual" and therefore Verboten!—unless, of course, the two people were a monogamously committed and married heterosexual couple, and even then . . .

Cloye expressed the modern view, popular with teenagers, that "sex" was pretty much limited to straight intercourse. Anything else was, at least morally, "no offsides, no foul." During the argument, as her mother's voice became louder and more strident, Cloye turned to her father for support. But Ramrod generally avoided getting involved in his wife's "Rules for Cloye and Doray."

Cloye flatly refused to accept her mother's view. No matter what her mother said, kissing boys was still okay. Even a little french kissing was still within bounds morally, no matter what their minister, Reverend Bill, said about the dangers of teenage dating.

Finally Ireme began crying and ran from the room.

Cloye thought the argument was over. Normally her mother would throw herself onto the sofa and scream, "My children are sending me to Hell!" Ireme would lie there, kicking her feet in the air and crying. This tantrum would go on until Ramrod would order Cloye to submit to her mother's rules. Cloye had seen this happen, over and over again, especially when Cloye found some excuse not to go to Mass, and later when she found some lame reason to avoid Ireme's new church.

Usually, during these arguments Cloye would stand next to the sofa and quietly explain—in a flat, rational tone—why her mother (and God) were wrong.

When, instead of screaming, her mother began crying and left the room, Cloye assumed that she had won the argument.

But then she discovered that her mother had enrolled her in a Christian college downstate. This was a real betrayal, in Cloye's view. Her mother had promised Cloye that she would have a say in where she went to college, and Cloye had hoped to go to Northern Illinois U. in DeKalb, or maybe even the University of Wisconsin.

Cloye and Ireme had recently gone to DeKalb to visit the campus of Northern. It was within a reasonable driving distance of their home in the Chicago suburbs, and the university had an excellent Art department. Ireme liked the fact that they refused to let alcohol on campus, but she was bothered by the fact that interracial dating was not discouraged—among the students it was even accepted!

Ireme wanted Cloye to go, instead, to a religious school and pushed hard for Cloye to attend Kansas Christians of Christ College. Ultimately, after listening to both sides, Ramrod made the final decision. Cloye would have to attend a Christian college in southern Illinois.

When Cloye told her friends, they were sympathetic. One said, "Good luck in The Land of the Pod People!"

Cloye wasn't sure what her friend meant by this—until she arrived at the school.

Forty years ago the school had mandated that all men wear ties and jackets, and all women wear skirts. That rule had recently fallen by the wayside. But even so, as Cloye drove on campus she noticed that many students still followed the old rules, and those who didn't were often wearing jeans and religious T-shirts. One football player wore a T-shirt with the image of a muscular Jesus doing push-ups. Most of the young men were either clean shaven with military-short hair or they wore Jesus-style beards and hairstyles. There were no tattoos, except a few crosses and other tattoos with a religious theme. The football player—who evidently shaved off all his body hair—had a tattoo that said "Pump up for Jesus."

The women were equally conventional. Some could have walked out of an advertisement printed in the 1950s. Most of the young women were neat and well groomed, with skirts that went well below the knee, and high heels. There were a few exceptions. Here and there she saw a Nashville type, with enormous blonde hair and a push-up bra. And, Cloye saw a few young women, slump shouldered, wearing blue jeans and shapeless blouses—trying their best to avoid looking too female.

As she pulled into a parking spot, Cloye could easily spot the faculty. Most of the men wore suits, with ties of course. A few of the Liberal Arts types (here called simply "Social Arts" to avoid the "liberal" label) wore denim slacks and sport jackets. Some even wore bow ties.

The women faculty, who were clearly in the minority, wore skirts and jackets. No woman dared to wear a pants suit, at least not on campus. The only exception to this rule was the Affirmative Action officer, an elderly woman who was probably a holdover from the '80s. She wore a brown pants suit, apparently as a statement of her power over the other administrators. She even smoked! In fact, she was at that moment standing outside the door of the Administration building smoking tiny little cigarillos. As Cloye watched, she made her statement of absolute power—tossing her cigarello butt to the concrete step and then crushing it under her heel.

As Cloye climbed out of her Buick, she noticed a huge banner

PREPARE FOR JESUS!

hanging draped across the dorm. This phrase seemed to be the current popular slogan in religious schools. In fact, this banner was left over from the nonalcoholic Millennium Party held on December 31st 1999, and it had only been brought out again as the date approached of Dr. Harold Cox's latest prediction for The Rapture and the beginning of The Last Days.

Cloye took her purse and the campus map and papers given to her at the gate, and she walked up to the dorm where she had been assigned. Because she had not been baptized as an adult, Cloye was assigned to the nonfundamentalist, nondenominational dormitory—along with the Mormons, Catholics, Seventh Day Adventists, New Agers, and the other "not real Christian" students.

Cloye got her room key at the front desk from a surly looking young black woman who usually worked for sub-minimum wage in the cafeteria. Cloye walked up the stairs, noting the '60s style architecture and the many religious slogans painted on the walls. There was a mural of Jesus, his hands bleeding from the iron nails driven through his palms, and the slogan:

HIS PAIN, YOUR GAIN

Along the halls were additional sketches and slogans:

PREPARE FOR JESUS

HE'S COMING AGAIN

WWYD
(What Would Yeshua Do?)

JESUS LOVES YOU, MAN!

As Cloye approached the door of her new room, she saw written on a banner:

"CHRIST CAN HEAL BODY AND SOUL"
—THE BIBLE—

Something about this bothered her. Cloye was used to her mother quoting Bible verses, but usually Ireme gave the chapter and verse, or at least the name of the book where it could be found. It seemed a bit odd to simply cite "The Bible" as a source. Maybe they were just making stuff up, or maybe they really didn't know where in the Bible it said this.

Cloye heard jazz coming from the end of the hall. She found the door standing open, and her new roommate—a short, stocky black woman—was sitting on one of the small beds. It was the "understood" rule of the college not to "mix the races" in a dormitory room;

but since this was the "not really Christian" dorm, the rule wasn't rigidly applied.

"Hi, I'm Minnie Ball," she said.

"I'm Cloye Steel," Cloye answered.

"Steel . . . Ball," Minnie said, "I guess that explains how they put us together."

"Yeah, just like Evil Knievel and Awful Knoffel."

Together they sorted out who had which bed, the closet space and the arrangement of clothes, shoes and coats. Minnie seemed like a nice girl, not overly bookish, and helpful in dealing with others. In fact, Minnie was originally from New Orleans, and she had been raised in the religion of Voudon, a mixture of Catholic and African beliefs.

Cloye continued to act as if she were vaguely religious, while Minnie set up a Voudon altar in the corner of her room. Unwilling to be seen as "different," Cloye announced herself to be "a sort of Catholic."

On Monday, Cloye started her classes. Academically, they were a step above high school, except for the Science classes which seemed pretty dumbed-down. On the first day of biology class, Cloye got her syllabus and her library Reserve Room reading list. The list of books that she was expected to read was pretty revealing. Under the heading "INTELLIGENT DESIGN" she found:

Science and Evolution: Developing a Christian Worldview of Science
Defeating Darwinism by Opening Minds: An Easy-to-Understand Guide
Battle for the Beginning: The Bible on Creationism and the Fall
Creation Hypothesis: Scientific Evidence for an Intelligent Designer
Dismantling Evolution: Building Intelligent Design
Tornado in a Junkyard: The Relentless Myth of Darwinism

This was only the beginning of a list that went on for several pages. The Honors students were expected to write a ten-page paper for the class, and they had to use these books as sources. Suddenly, Cloye was glad not to be an Honors student. But, like other non-Honors students, Cloye had to write a one-page book report on one of these books.

Out of curiosity, Cloye went to the library and checked out a copy of *Tornado in a Junkyard*. The author, Mr. Perloff, stated up front that he was not a scientist. Cloye was impressed with his honesty, and she began skimming through his book. Cloye thought it was a bit odd, but Mr. Perloff spent a whole chapter trying to prove that the play *Inherit the Wind*, which is based on the Scopes Monkey Trial, was not an accurate portrayal of the historic trial. Cloye was not sure why this was so important to Mr. Perloff. After all, a play is a dramatic work and there was no reason to believe that the authors were trying to create an accurate blow-by-blow recreation of the Scopes Trial. It seemed to Cloye that Mr. Perloff was focusing on the wrong issues. And what did this have to do with biology or evolution? Cloye was confused. Mr. Perloff seemed to think that if the play was wrong about history, then Evolution had to be wrong, too.

The Introduction to Physics & Earth Sciences class was even more odd. The professor used a textbook, approved by the State of Texas, which had been cleansed of any unChristian ideas about the origins of the earth. The textbook dealt with the bare facts of rocks and minerals, without any speculation about the age of the earth or the age of dinosaur bones. The author of the textbook was from Colorado Springs, where Cloye and her family had vacationed the previous summer.

During their vacation in Colorado, Cloye had seen several fossil displays, and on the way back they had stopped at a museum in Kansas. The museum had thousands of fossilized shark teeth that had been found in the eastern plains of Colorado and in Kansas, all from a time millions of years ago when both states had been submerged under a prehistoric sea. Cloye knew that, if the author of the text was from Colorado, he had to be aware of this. It bothered her that the author of the text was avoiding any facts that might raise questions in the minds of the students. On the other hand, the textbook was illustrated with several funny B.C. cartoons, which showed that men and dinosaurs could live together in harmony.

For Cloye, however, the worst was yet to come.

On her first day of class, Cloye walked into the art studio and found a group of "popular" students chatting about the importance of joining a "good Christian" sorority. They ignored Cloye when she entered the room and continued their chatter about frat parties and sneaking alcohol into the dorms.

One of the girls was going on and on about the frat party she had gone to the night before:

"Yeah, I went upstairs looking for Laura and I opened the door to her boyfriend's room. She wasn't there, so I went to the bathroom and, Holy Crap, there they were. She was on all fours puking into the toilet. And he was pulling her hair and doing her, doggie style.

"Really?"

"Yeah, I couldn't believe it."

"Wow, I've never seen anyone on the receiving end of a Santorum before!"

"Yeah, too bad you missed it. It was gross!"

"I think I'd have to be really, really drunk for that."

"Sure you would. Me, too."

And so on. Cloye tried to ignore them. The sorority girls were really not much different from the cheeleaders back in high school. Cloye had avoided them, too. It didn't take Cloye long to realize that the most vulgar girls were, of course, the PKs (Preachers' Kids) who did drugs, a lot, and liked to perform sex acts in public places—especially churches. The sorority girls may have been gross, but the PKs were downright nasty. Cloye had met dozens of PKs at church camp, and they were all very damaged people. Cloye was caught between feelings of pity and revulsion.

In the middle of this public confession, Professor Wyatt, a thirty-ish young man with a Jesus-style beard and long (but conservatively so) hairstyle, finally appeared. He entered the room with a grand flourish as if he were the reincarnation of Michelangelo. He wore blue jeans—and not the brand new, fashionable style either. Instead he wore faded old jeans with a patch over one knee. He didn't wear a regular shirt, but instead wore a T-shirt which, amazingly enough, had paint stains but no religious slogans.

Cloye didn't pay too much attention to Professor Wyatt, who was preoccupied with chatting up the sorority girls. Instead she looked at the many paintings and sketches on the walls, along with photographs of sculpture. Most were by former students. But the artwork fell into two general categories: still life sketches and religious art.

This was how Professor Wyatt organized the class. Mediocre artists were encouraged to do still life sketches, while the more talented students were "commissioned" to do religious art.

After seeing one of her sketches, Wyatt decided to "commission" Cloye. For her first project, Cloye decided to paint her roommate Minnie.

This proved to be a mistake.

Professor Wyatt stood behind Cloye while she started an outline of the painting. He said, "Oh, you're going to attempt a portrait?"

"Yes," Cloye said.

"A painting of Jesus?"

"No."

"An Apostle, Paul perhaps?"

"No."

Cloye could hear the subtle change in his breathing as Professor Wyatt moved on to another student.

A few minutes later Professor Wyatt returned. By now Cloye's painting was showing a definite female form.

"Ah, a portrait of the Madonna?"

"The pop singer?" Cloye said, just to get his reaction.

"Pop singer? No, I meant Mary, the mother of Jesus."

"Oh, no—it's not Mary. And it's not Madonna either."

"Really? Your student record shows that you were raised a Catholic, so I assumed you might want to do a Madonna, or perhaps a saint."

"No, not really. I'm not doing a religious painting."

Professor Wyatt snorted, stared at the picture for a few minutes, then wandered away again.

As the days passed, Professor Wyatt seemed distant. He would clearly have preferred that Cloye do a still life rather than a portrait of Minnie, but she ignored his hints.

After a few days, the painting clearly began to resemble Minnie. Slowly word got around that Cloye's painting was of her black roommate.

And this is how the scandal began.

In Professor Wyatt's art class it was okay to do a religious painting, or you could do a painting of a family member, or a guy could paint his girlfriend (if done tastefully), or a girl could paint her boyfriend (if he wasn't a complete troll). But for a guy to paint a guy, or a girl to paint a girl—well, this wasn't encouraged.

Both Cloye and Minnie seemed oblivious to the growing scandal. Even when one of the girls in their dorm wrote the phrase "rug-munch room" on their door, it didn't seem to sink in with Cloye or Minnie. Cloye went on with her painting, and Minnie continued to make and sell love charms to the other girls in the dorm.

Eventually the Housing Office notified Cloye that a new room was available, at no extra charge, if she wanted to have her own private place.

Cloye moved into the new room and enjoyed the extra space.

This seemed to defuse the problem, at least for a while.

When her painting was finished, Professor Wyatt looked it over carefully, made several encouraging noises, and then gave Cloye a B+ for the project. At the same time he gave several sorority girls A and A+ grades for their paintings and even for the still life sketches that showed little real talent or effort.

As her second project Cloye decided to go with the flow. She started work on a wooden crucifix and did her best to finish the job quickly. Some of her music classes were demanding, and so she decided not to waste too much time on a project that would probably only get her a B+ at best.

Cloye nailed together two sticks of wood, making a large cross about 3' by 5' tall, and then she painted a rough-looking Jesus on the cross. The crucifix had an interesting "primitive" look and Professor Wyatt even stopped to compliment her efforts. Cloye cut the bottom off a 3 pound can of coffee and nailed it on the back of the cross as a kind of halo, which impressed her teacher and resulted in even more compliments, including a few from the other students. Finally Cloye added a strand of barbed wire to the crucifix, wrapping it from top to bottom in tightly wound steel.

When it was finished, Professor Wyatt suggested that Cloye submit her crucifix to the Oktoberfest Art Contest—a contest that he himself judged.

Cloye was flattered by the attention and submitted the crucifix to the contest.

The day of the contest Professor Wyatt gave Cloye's crucifix an "Honorable Mention" ribbon.

First Prize went to an acrylic paint-on-velvet portrait of Reverend Bob, the founder of the college. He and his wife were portrayed as standing with Jesus between them, embracing the both of them. The painting had an eerie kind of "American Gothic" look to it, except without the pitchfork.

Second Prize went to a Nativity scene. The animals in the manger were made of clay, and the figures also served as a serving set: The cow was a gravy boat, the ox was a sugar bowl, and the three Wise

Men were salt, pepper, and Tabasco sauce. A fourth figure, apparently three shepherds joined at the waist, was used as a mustard pot. Several other animals were included, and even a drummer boy. His drum served as a toothpick holder.

Third Prize went to a painting of the Madonna. In the portrait, Mary was surrounded by abortion protestors, and carrying signs that read, “Let your baby live” and “abortion kills.” The artist made a point of telling everyone who would listen that the historic Mary did not have blue eyes, but she could have had blue eye shadow and a little Egyptian mascara.

Fourth prize went to a crucifix made entirely out of plastic roses. One of the sorority sisters decided to “borrow” Cloye's idea and made a 4' x 4' cross of white roses with blood-colored plastic roses stuck on the spots where the hands and feet would have been.

Cloye was glad to have her work recognized, but she was puzzled too. She found Professor Wyatt and asked him why her crucifix was not as good as the rosy cross that won Fourth Prize.

“Why, my dear, the reason is obvious,” he said. “When you painted Jesus on The Cross, you portrayed Him with the nail wounds on His hands. This is obviously a mistake. Historians and scholars have proven that Jesus’ wounds were above His wrists, not in His hands.”

“His wrists?” Cloye was stunned. Every crucifix she had ever seen, in every Catholic Church she had entered, all had the iron nails driven through Christ’s hands.

“Yes, of course,” he said. “But a nail driven through the palm of the hand would tear out, once you put weight on it. The Roman soldiers had to drive the nail between the bones above His wrist for it to hold under the weight of Christ’s body. Obviously, this is a minor error, but it was enough to cost you a prize.”

Cloye stood silent for a moment. “But doesn’t the Gospel of John say that when the resurrected Christ came to the apostles, he showed them the wounds in his hands?”

Professor Wyatt shook his head, “I’m sure that is a misreading of the text. But your mistake is not a serious one. What is more troubling is that you forgot the sign.”

“What sign?”

“When Christ was crucified, the Romans put a sign on the cross, over His head. The sign read ‘Jesus, King of the Jews.’”

“I can add a sign,” Cloye said.

"Yes, of course you can, but it is too late to affect the awarding of prizes. I'm sorry." Professor Wyatt shook his head, sympathetically, as he walked away.

Cloye went back to her room, but the more she thought about it the angrier she got. She had played along with Professor Wyatt's Bible trivia game, and she'd come out with the short end of the stick.

And then she got an idea.

Cloye went to the student health center and got a suppository for severe constipation.

The next morning the prize-winning art works were moved to a display at Oktoberfest. Cloye went to the display and found her crucifix.

The wooden crucifix was in the prize section with three other "Honorable Mention" awards. But Cloye's crucifix clearly stood out as the best of them. The primitive wood and barbed wire crucifix was cleverly done, and the painting on the wood showed a certain style that was absent from the other works. The circle of shining metal—the "halo"—was imaginative use of basic, everyday materials.

Cloye took a "Prepare for Jesus!" banner from the front door of the exhibit room and then draped it over the wall where her crucifix was hanging.

Cloye took the round sticker she removed from the suppository box and applied it to the metal disk. The sticker read:

Warning: Prepare rectum before inserting product

Later that day, when the art exhibit opened, all hell broke loose. Several people suggested that Professor Wyatt be fired for giving an award to a sacrilegious art work. As soon as she heard about this, Cloye went to the Chairman of the Art Department and confessed that she had "altered" the crucifix without Professor Wyatt's knowledge.

Cloye was expelled from the college.

Within an hour she had packed her things and had started driving back toward Chicago, on highway 55.

* * *

That afternoon, Capt. Ramrod, Jesus, and Hadshe D. were the last to exit the 747. They could see Mark Doody scampering along in the distance, trying his best to outrun the other passengers and get to the terminal first. Jesus produced his infamous "Beavis and Butthead remote control" (designed to look like a television remote control) from his flight jacket and pointed it toward Mark. He pressed a button, and an electronic "Boom!" could be heard coming from the device.

Ramrod thought Jesus' little game was a bit too juvenile, but Hadshe encouraged him.

"Use the 'slap' button!"she said.

Jesus pointed the remote control at Mark and said, "And now God smites the unbeliever!" pressing the button. A loud "Smack!" came from the plastic remote.

At that moment Mark tripped over an uneven piece of concrete and fell flat on his face. Jesus looked at the remote, then at Mark.

"It works! Jesus smites the unbeliever!"

Ramrod got his pilot's cap and fitted it over his manly scalp. He was proud of the fact that his hairline had not yet begun to recede. And there was only the slightest touch of gray in his hair, just enough to give him a distinguished look. On the other hand, it did remind him of the age difference between himself and Hadshe.

As they watched, Jesus jumped onto the plastic slide and was swiftly carried to the ground. Hadshe looked at Ramrod and said, "Age before beauty."

Ramrod grimaced, then said, "Ladies first."

Hadshe stepped onto the chute and disappeared.

Ramrod pulled his cap tighter and stepped after her.

At the bottom of the chute, a golf cart pulled up. The driver smiled at Hadshe and said, "Room for one more."

"Let's both go!" Hadshe laughed, as she maneuvered Ramrod into the empty seat. And then she slid onto his lap.

For Ramrod this was like a dream come true (sorry, it was a dream come true). Here he was with the de-licktable, delightfully delectable Hadshe Dunhim on his lap, her firm but ample buttocks planted on his lap, her perky breasts bouncing with each bump of the ride. From here Ramrod could smell her perfume, and below the perfume the scent of her . . . it was just too much. It was more than he could believe, and a silent prayer—"Thank you God!"—came from his lips. At the next bump, he put his hands around her waist and hugged her tight.

Hadshe laughed at Jesus as they passed him, and in minutes she and Ramrod were at the terminal gate, ready to go up the stairs.

Hadshe lingered just a bit as she dismounted Ramrod's groin, and she even gave him a last bump and grind as she slipped off his lap. For his part, Ramrod was excited by the pressure of Hadshe's flesh and yet felt a little guilty for the pleasure it gave him.

There was, still, in the back of his mind, the worry about what lay ahead. Were people being taken up to Heaven, one by one, as the rest of humanity was "left behind"? His dream—or rather the nightmare he'd had on board the 747—still lingered, along with the unexplained fear that his wife, Ireme, and their children might be gone forever, called to Heaven by God.

Could The Rapture have happened?

Could The Rapture be happening, even now?

FOUR

Mr. Mark "Barky Bark" Doody picked up his battered laptop and wandered toward the airport terminal, but now he had a bruised knee and a noticeable limp. The pain only served to remind him of the deliciously beautiful Hadshe. Each jab of pain was like the pleasure Mark felt in remembering just exactly how she had placed her hand in his pants pocket. It would be fair to say that Mark's soul was filled with the conviction that (1) Hadshe bore a striking resemblance to Australian supermodel Kim Hiott, and (2) that—because of his fabulous jet-set aura—Hadshe was very deeply in love with him. And, even more unlikely, Mark believed that by helping Hadshe's career he would soon be dating her on a regular basis. Mark believed that, even though she was taller than he was, they would make a great "power couple" among the "beautiful people" in Hollywood and New York. Mark understood that they might never be as famous as Tiger Woods and Kim Hiott—who had been romantically attached in today's gossip column in *Weekly Whirled News*. But you never know.

Mark reached the terminal, well ahead of the other passengers, and found a wireless hookup for his laptop. He wanted to check his e-mail and see if there was any more news coming out of the United

Nations about Nickelay Dubyah, who was about to be nominated "Fearless Leader" of the country of Texrectumstan.

As he paged through dozens of e-mails offering the latest "Ancient Chinese secrets for penis enlargement" Mark stumbled across an e-mail from his boss, Stone Bord, the editor of *Weekly Whirled News*. Mark almost missed this message, buried as it was among the messages from Nigerian government officials offering millions of dollars to anyone who would help them get their stolen millions out of Nigerian banks and safely to banks in the USA. Mark had tried to help these poor souls on three or four occasions, but in each case the Nigerian officials had taken Mark's money and left nothing in the account he had opened! Mark was seriously miffed at these people for abusing his trust. Even worse were the offers for online casinos and dozens of escort services (at least four or five of which Mark had never—as best he could remember—done business with).

Mark assumed that all this e-mail was due to the fact that he was a world traveler and that, as such, he was going to be bombarded with erotic e-mails from "willing Russian ladies," "hot Polish chicks with big Polish sausages," and "obese Italian grannies." The company Information Systems officer had warned Mark more than once that he was using too much space in the server for junk e-mail. But Mark was unwilling to pay for a separate e-mail account at home, and so his personal life—such as it was—often spilled over into his business e-mail account.

Mark opened the e-mail from Stone Bord, his Editor in Chief, and skipped on past the usual threats about overpriced massages on his expense account. Down toward the end of the message he found the information he wanted. It was a short bio of Nickelay Dubyah and his father, Nickelay the Elder. The article, imitating the sardonic style of Lush Rimbaugh, was written by the obituary editor at WWN:

> Nickelay the Elder has served for fifteen years as Fearless Leader, Dictator, and Supreme Commander of the former Soviet republic of Texrectumstan. Earlier in his career, Nickelay rose in the provincial government and eventually he became head of the Secret Police. Shortly after the fall of the Soviet Empire, he seized control of the government in a bloody coup and began ruling with an iron fist (actually a titanium golf club). Nickelay the Elder was

on good terms with most of the dictators in the region, and he was on especially good terms with Sodom Hussein of Iraq, with whom he frequently golfed, drank, and swapped mistresses.

This came to an abrupt end when Nickelay caught Sodom cheating to shave points on his golf game. Nickelay had, over the years, lost millions of dollars to Sodom in their monthly golf outings, and so Nickelay felt entitled to retaliate against his old friend. Nickelay the Elder invaded the country of Iraq and tried to assassinate his former friend and ally, Sodom. Unfortunately, Nickelay the Elder missed killing Sodom, but he did manage to capture his son Uday Hussein. Nickelay personally shot Uday in both legs with a .45, and then said, "That'll keep you off the goddamn golf course!" and "Tell your old man ''ll catch up with him later!"

The Arabic news channel, All Jizz Erah, televised the story of how Nickelay the Elder had attempted to assassinate Sodom. This story was flashed all across the world. Soon Nickelay became known as "The Butcher of Baghdad" for the way he brutally shot his old friend's son, Uday. Nickelay the Elder also seized millions of dollars skimmed from Iraqi oil profits as reparations for all the millions he had lost in golf games.

His son, Nickelay Dubyah (pronounced "Dub-Yah") the Younger, is the last and least of Nickelay the Elder's many illegitimate children. Dubyah's mother was Nickelay's favorite mistress, which led to young Dubyah becoming the favored target for his older siblings' resentment.

Growing up, young Dubyah had to deal with the usual teasing and bullying from his older half-brothers and sisters, many of whom now have full-time jobs working in the copper mines of his native Texrectumstan. As Dubyah grew up, there were also the inevitable assassination attempts; but Dubyah seems to be some kind of human cockroach in his ability to escape certain death. His siblings have tried car bombs, poison, hit men, hit women, and even a few exploding camels—but so far they haven't been able to tag him. Except for a few small bruises and scars, and a few dozen serious brain concussions, Dubyah has escaped unscathed. The latest attempt, a grenade attack in 1997, left Dubyah the Younger with a steel plate in his head.

Luckily for him, in 1998 his mother staged a wedding where the elder Nickelay thought he was to be the Best Man. Instead, the marriage turned out to be for him. This weird plan actually succeeded, in part because the elder Nickelay was inebriated and the effect of tertiary syphilis had rotted his brain to the point that he

> didn't know where he was anyway. Under Texrectumstanian law, this marriage made Dubyah the Younger the only illegitimate (but legal) heir to all his father's lands and titles.
>
> Today Nickelay Dubyah the Younger appears to be in line for an executive position with the United Nations and appointments to the World Bank, the International Monetary Fund, and perhaps even the Presidency of the New World Order.

Mark puzzled over this information. He was especially intrigued by the idea that a man as powerful and influential as Nickelay Dubyah the Younger would be interested in running a private enterprise like the New World Order, a worldwide sports entertainment conglomerate. All that Mark knew about the N.W.O. was that it controlled all of the professional wrestling matches around the world (even in Texrectumstan). Mark had trouble visualizing a man like Nickelay hanging out with a bunch of sweaty wrestlers, but then, he thought, "Hey, whatever turns your crank."

* * *

When he got to his car, a sleek silver Lexus, Ramrod Steel turned on the radio to listen to the news. Ramrod knew that the secular news media wouldn't want to admit that The Rapture had happened. Ireme was always telling Ramrod about the anti-christian bias of the liberal media. Ireme said that when The Rapture finally happened, the news media would try to cover it up. So Ramrod listened very carefully to the news reports.

Maybe there was some clue, some news report that would hint at The Rapture. Ramrod listened closely as the newscaster told of six corpses that had disappeared from a morgue in Chicago. The radio commentator suggested that perhaps they had gone out to vote. Then there was a news story about a nine-year-old boy who had disappeared from his front yard the day before. And there was another story about a man from Rockford who had disappeared from a cruise ship near Saint Croix. In New Rochelle a woman had disappeared, along with her children, and the police assumed that she was running away from her estranged husband—but was she? Ramrod visualized the mother and children disappearing in the wink of an eye—called to Heaven by God! Perhaps it was really happening, just like Dr. Harold Cox had said it would.

Agitated, Ramrod drove to his house in the suburbs, a little known real estate development called Mt. Saint Mary, and quickly reached his two-storey home at the end of a long circle drive. The neighborhood seemed to be in a state of disarray. Along the street there were at least three lawns that needed mowing, two yards had bushes that needed a serious trim, and the house next to his had a beat up old 1964 Ford parked in the drive—in plain view!

"You'd think the jerks would have the decency to think about property values and put that heap of junk in their garage!" Ramrod muttered to himself.

Ramrod had stopped earlier at a gas station and called home on his cell phone. All he got was Ireme's voice on the answering machine:

"We can't come to the phone right now. Leave a message and we'll get back to you, unless we are taken up in The Rapture. So if we don't call back, you understand it's not that your call isn't important to us. But we must answer to a Higher Power." This was followed by the "beep" and an eerie silence.

The sound of Ireme's voice nearly brought tears to Ramrod's eyes. She was such a kind woman, so cheerful and so giving . . . and especially giving. Ireme did more for charity than anyone else he ever knew. Ramrod had to buy a steel cabinet with a lock in order to protect his sports equipment and his power tools. Even the riding lawn-mower had a bicycle lock on it. Ireme simply couldn't be trusted with anything of value. It was like living with a drug addict, because expensive household items tended to disappear after a few weeks. Ramrod was surprised that Ireme hadn't (yet) hocked her wedding ring and given the money away to religious charities.

Ramrod climbed out of the Lexus and walked to the front door. It was locked, as Ramrod thought it might be. Ramrod was convinced that Ireme had been carried away to Heaven in the night. So, of course, the front door would still be locked. He bent over and picked up the newspaper. "At least the paperboy is still here," he thought.

Unlocking the door, he entered the foyer, where he put his pilot's cap and jacket into the front closet. There was a distinctive smell in the air, a leftover from the many times Ireme had burnt dinner because she was praying on her knees, in the middle of a Novena. She would rather burn the food than break off her prayers, because this would have been a serious breach of etiquette with God.

Ramrod sniffed at the faint hint of charred meat and thought, "She always treated me like a god." Again a faint tear began to form in the corner of his eye.

Climbing the stairs, he could hear the clock radio in his bedroom, tuned to the Christian radio station that Ireme liked so much. "You are now listening to KDOGG, the voice of Christian radio." This message was followed by a set of unidentifiable tunes, each one extolling the love of God, sacrifice, submission, and charity. Then the music was interrupted by an evangelist asking for donations of money to buy powdered milk "for the destitute families of diamond miners in Darkest Africa."

As he reached the top of the stairs, Ramrod saw that the door was ajar to his son Doray's room. His mind wandered back to that day, twelve years ago—the day Doray was born—and how proud he was to be the father of a bouncing baby boy. "Look at those feet!" Dr. Probosco had said, "He's going to be a football player for sure!" Ramrod was disappointed that his son had grown up, instead, to lead the Pep Squad. It was just one more disappointment in his life. Ramrod had wanted a Quarterback, and instead life had turned him into a Mascot. On the bedstead was a photo of Doray in his animal outfit—he was the mascot for the famous "Fighting Squirrels" of Mt. Saint Mary High School. Doray was in the center of the photo, the kid holding the enormous nuts.

There were, of course, other better memories that Ramrod held dear. His son had been active in Boy Scouts. Over the years Doray had attained practically every badge and award that a scout could get. He had recently become an Eagle Scout through their new church. And Doray had even been selected to present the scout troop's highest award to former First Lady Barbara Bush when she came to Chicago. It was a moment of great pride for both Ireme and Ramrod, watching their son present the prestigious "Silver Beaver Award" to the former First Lady. The entire family, except for Cloye, was included in a photo which was published in the local shopper's guide.

There was certainly both the good and the bad in Ramrod's life, but all in all he was mostly happy that his son had achieved at least some minor recognition in life. Ramrod, of course, hoped that Doray might also, someday, join the US Air Force and become a pilot. Unfortunately, Doray showed more interest in the Navy than he did in the Air Force, and if he ever did become a pilot, he would be a

Navy pilot. This idea bothered Ramrod, who thought Navy pilots were a bunch of second-rate bums.

Ramrod walked up to his son's bed. He could see Doray's new Nikes, sticking out from under the bed, and his clothes were laid out on a chair. "These are the clothes he would have worn to school, today," Ramrod thought. And, as Ramrod walked over to the bed, he knew what he would find.

There was a slight indentation on Doray's pillow.

"That was where his head was lying, when God took him to Heaven," Ramrod whispered to himself. Next to the pillow was Doray's teddy bear. "He was probably wearing his 'Jesus Loves Me' pajamas last night," Ramrod said. He knew that, when he pulled back the covers, the pajamas would be all that was left, as Doray had already been taken up in The Rapture.

It was more than he could bear, his trembling fingers touching the edge of the blanket. "It's probably best just to pull the blanket back." But he knew what he would find.

His hand gripped the blanket tightly, and he pulled it to one side. There, lying on the sheet, was a white sports bra.

"What the hell!"

He pulled back on the blanket a bit more and found, in the middle of the bed, a pair of girl's white cotton briefs. Ramrod stepped back, his universe shaken by this discovery.

"What the hell was Cloye doing sleeping in Doray's bed?" he said, to no one in particular. "And where the hell are Doray's pajamas?"

From here Ramrod made his way to the Master Bedroom. As he passed along the hallway, he felt as if he were being watched. Then he realized it was just the plaster figurines in the hall display case. In the hallway was the case full of Precocious Minutes collectible plates. Ramrod had given Ireme a new plate every Christmas, on the kids' birthdays, on her birthday and on Mother's Day. Most of the more valuable plates were missing, sold for cash that was sent to Christian charities. But since the plates had been gifts, Ramrod tried not to complain about what Ireme did with them.

He entered the bedroom slowly, his mind wandering back to those days, long ago, when they were first married. Ireme's father had paid thousands of dollars so that she could have a full-out Catholic wedding. They even got married in the cathedral, back in the days before Ireme turned her back on The Church and her conservative Catholic upbringing.

The various saints' pictures and religious icons were all gone now. Ireme had gotten rid of it all. She had become a Charismatic Catholic briefly, but then she stopped going to Mass and instead joined a local Evangelical church.

After moving from a Catholic to a Protestant church, her taste in home décor changed, too. Now their bedroom was decorated with Precocious Minutes prints, wallpaper, and lamps. Even the old bedroom set had been replaced with a modern "Precocious Minutes Oak Masters" bedstead. Each of the bedposts was carved with a Precocious Minutes figure—a child with huge vacant eyes and a bulbous head.

As Ramrod walked through the bedroom, his fingers lightly touched Ireme's possessions. On the dresser was her box of costume jewelry, mostly plain nickel-plated Crosses. Ramrod knew that nothing was left of her ornate gold crucifixes or her more expensive jewelry, and even the inlaid jewelry box was missing. Their wedding picture in the antique silver frame was also gone.

Ramrod walked over to their bed and found, on the floor, Ireme's white flannel nightgown lying in a heap beside the bed. He reached down to pick it up, and lying underneath the nightgown were her fuzzy bedroom slippers and her white lacy cotton undies. It was clear-Ireme had been taken up to Heaven while she was saying her prayers, down on her knees beside the bed.

Shattered, Ramrod picked up the clothing and fell to the bed, pressing the soft cloth to his face in order to inhale, one last time, the smell that was, to his shattered mind, all that was left behind of his beloved wife.

* * *

At the same moment that Ramrod Steel was lying on his bed, wandering through long lost memories of Ireme, who had been taken up to Heaven in The Rapture, this same Ireme and their son Doray were on a Greyhound bus heading south toward Saint Louis, Missouri.

After twenty years of marriage, Ireme Steel had decided that she could no longer stay married to an Unbeliever. The last two years had been almost unbearable, as Ramrod ignored her faith in God, ignored her love for Jesus, and resented the time and money she spent on her church and on her religious charity work.

She had already lost her only daughter Cloye to Satan, and she was afraid it was only a matter of time before Doray was lost forever, too. She had to get Doray away from the evil influence of his father and his sister.

Ireme didn't want to leave a goodbye note. She just wanted to disappear.

She hocked her wedding ring and all that was left of her good jewelry. She took all the cash she could get together from various credit cards. She decided to take Doray to a real Christian community. There her most cherished values would be the same Real American values held by all good Christians.

And so she and Doray were now on their way to Branson, Missouri.

FIVE

From the window of the Greyhound bus, Ireme could see that they were getting closer and closer to Missouri. As the bus neared East Saint Louis, she saw a sign for Cahokia, a pagan religious site built by the prehistoric heathen Indians, along with a place called Woodhenge (like Stonehenge, except made out of wood). Ireme could imagine the pagan fertility rituals, the sacrificed virgins, and the obscene Satan-inspired beliefs of these ancient Native Americans. The more she thought about it, the more horrified she became. Many questions fired through her head.

Why didn't the early Christian settlers destroy the Indian mounds?

Why did the Catholic priests, who settled here, build a monastery on the ancient pyramid instead of destroying it?

Why did the United Nations think it was important to preserve this evil place?

Why haven't they built a casino here yet?

All these ideas and more washed through Ireme's fevered brain. Most of what she knew about Indians she had learned from her father, who had grown up in Spooner, Wisconsin. Her father often said that the local tribe (called "Little Ears" by the French explorers) was made up of lazy, no good bums who lay around all day and lived off of government welfare checks. They were always complaining about how the White Men had stolen their lands.

Worse yet, these Indians had all sorts of special privileges that the Federal Government preserved for them, alone.

First, they could gather wild rice from the lake.

Second, they could gather cranberries from the lake.

Third, they could spearfish on the lake.

Ireme's father, who ran a hunting lodge outside of Spooner, had complained bitterly about all these special rights and privileges. He was especially incensed about the Indians' spearfishing rights, since this cut into the stock of fish in the lake and his ability to attract wealthy sports fishermen from Chicago. After a poor season, he would drink heavily, lie around the house and grouse about the shortage of fish. Once he was thoroughly drunk, he would start yelling, "Why don't those red bastards move down to Eau Claire and open a casino!"

And so Ireme was puzzled, too, about how a tribe of Indians could simply die out like that, leaving behind enormous pyramids and wooden structures and nothing else.

"Why didn't they just go on Food Stamps?" she thought.

* * *

Mark's knee still ached from the fall. He had pulled himself up from the cracked concrete and his hand shot to his groin to make sure there were no serious injuries. As Chris the flight attendant walked past and shot a look at Mark. Mark, with his hand still on his groin, muttered, "just checking."

His mind kept wandering back to the beautiful Hadshe Dunhim and the sensation of her delicate hand slipping into his pants pocket. He had already forgotten about the business card and the fact that the only reason her hand was in his pocket was that she wanted something from him.

Soon Mark was eating lunch at the 1st Class Club where he could hook up his laptop and check the rest of his e-mail. He ignored the 37 messages from "Russian Brides" and went directly to an e-mail from Richard Burton who used the code name "The Welshman." Richard was a well connected source deeply embedded in the East European headquarters of the New World Order. The message was only one line long, but it was enough to make the hairs on the back of Mark's neck stand to attention. It read: "They have re-opened the bio-warfare lab in Africa."

This was very, very bad. Everything Lucy had said was coming true.

Mark's mind wandered back to the night before, the hotel in England and his escort, Lucy Washington. Mark had been in London for several days, and—as he usually did—Mark had sought out the professional services of Lucy, who ran a Christian escort service.

That night Lucy and Mark went to an expensive restaurant. Soon Mark was shoveling steak and onions into his mouth, while Lucy talked. And talked.

Lucy had just finished explaining her theory of how to run a "Jesus oriented" escort service.

"And you should always let me know when you're in town," she said, pressing her heavy bosoms together. "I'd always make time to have dinner with a fine looking white boy like you."

Mark said, "This is the first time I've been in London, at least since last January when I interviewed Sir Elton."

"Oh, I just love Elton, and his candle song. I tear up every time I hear it. I can't help it. I just tear up."

"Well get ready to tear up again. I have a copy of his CD back in my hotel room."

Miss Lucy's hand slipped across the table and she squeezed Mark's hand with a delicate pressure on his Love Line.

Miss Lucy was from Liberia, and she was willing and able to engage in any physical act that you could imagine—as long as it didn't involve straight intercourse. Lucy worked hard to support her ailing mother back in Liberia, not to mention an upscale apartment, a wardrobe of designer labels, and a collection of shoes that could make a Madonna jealous.

Miss Lucy considered herself a Missionary of God's Love, and she preached her love of Jesus to everyone she met. She was also very particular to tithe exactly 10% of her income (after taxes) to the Church of England.

Her real name was not, of course, Lucy Washington. But she did tell all the Americans she met that she was a direct descendant of the First President of the U.S. of A. This was, of course, just a story she made up for her clients. Ironically, she was from a family of slaves owned by President George Washington, and directly descended from George's father by way of a freed slave who emigrated to Liberia in 1811. So Lucy was, in reality, George's very distant (and very black) cousin.

But, as far as she knew, Lucy's only direct connection to George Washington was the fact that her cleavage was as awe inspiring as Valley Forge. And so she leaned forward again, to display it for Mark.

"Mark, what are you doing here in London? Are you interviewing Elton again?"

"No, I'm following up a lead. A friend of mine. He's kind of a conspiracy nut. He thinks that a secret cabal is preparing to conquer the world. My friend really does believe in this stuff, and he publishes a newsletter here in London."

"Oh, you must mean Richard Burton."

Mark started, and his face blanched whiter than it already was.

"You know Richard?"

"Yes, Dick the Welshman."

"Yes . . . he is Welsh," Mark stammered.

"Of course his real name isn't Burton. That's just an alias. But he is Welsh. He's been a fan of the actor Richard Burton ever since he saw the movie *The Spy Who Came in from the Cold*. And that's why he uses the name Richard Burton, or Dick the Welshman."

"So you know Dick, . . . intimately?"

"Sure, I just saw him last Thursday. I was telling him all about my dreams. And how The Antichrist was coming. I saw it all in a dream."

"So you told Dick about The Antichrist."

"Yes, of course."

Mark leaned back in his chair; the glass of wine shook in his hand. "And what exactly did you tell Dick about The Antichrist?"

"Well, it's like this," she said. "Most people think that The Antichrist is going to be a popular political figure: handsome, intelligent, charismatic. They think he'll be just like Tony Blair."

"And you don't agree?"

"No. I think that The Antichrist is going to slip in on us. We won't even know he's coming. He won't be smart, or intelligent, or charismatic."

"He won't."

"No, he won't. When The Antichrist comes, he'll be a smirking, swaggering boob. He'll have all the brains and charisma of a used car salesman."

Mark downed the last of his wine, then poured another. And in those few moments his mind kicked into gear briefly, and he thought about Nickelay Dubyah the Younger. Could Nickelay Dubyah be The Antichrist? Could he be the Embodiment of Pure (more or less) Evil?

"It's just like Hannah Arendt said about the Holocaust." Lucy smiled over her soufflé. "It's the Mediocrity of Evil. That's why Evil succeeds. It slips past us because we won't recognize it. We refuse to see it. Until it runs us over."

"Don't you mean 'The banality of evil'?"

"Banality, mediocrity, whatever! He'll have all those qualities, and more. Just wait for when The Antichrist comes. He'll devour the world and then crap it out, big as life, right on prime time television. And no one will say boo about it."

* * *

You could see it from the signs along the highway. In Illinois there were signs about DeKalb Corn, signs for restaurants, signs for gas stations. Ireme saw the signs change as the bus passed over the bridge going into Missouri. There were dozens of signs for Branson, and many signs along the highway carried religious messages, including a sign at least sixty feet across that read:

A MAN WHO PUTS AWAY HIS WIFE AND
TAKES ANOTHER COMMITS ADULTERY

For just a moment, Ireme thought about Ramrod. Or, more specifically, about Ramrod's physical needs. Would Ramrod be able to give up sex and live a celibate life now that he no longer had a wife? Ireme struggled with this idea for three or four seconds, then quickly put it out of her mind. She could not take responsibility for her husband's future sins. From now on, he was on his own.

And as they got even closer to their destination, turning down highway 65 toward Branson, she saw plenty of signs for businesses selling Precocious Minutes figurines, Precocious Minutes greeting cards, and at least a dozen signs for the Precocious Minutes Angelic Messages phone cards. Each plastic phone card had, embossed on the surface, a picture of the Precocious Minutes Angel talking into a cloud-shaped pay phone.

Ireme decided that she had to get a job working in the Precocious Minutes Theme Park in Branson, even if it meant working for sub-minimum wage in a fast food restaurant.

Doray had fallen asleep, still wearing his "I Love Jesus" pajamas and a pair of flip flops. His cherubic face reminded Ireme of the Precocious Minutes figures, their enormous eyes (which the Chinese workers hand painted and had so much trouble with), their too-white skin, and their enigmatic smiles. Ireme wanted her son to grow up to be just like these figurines: fragile, pretty, and very, very white.

* * *

Mark sat at the table of a small pub in London. Sitting across from him was the enigmatic figure of Dick the Welshman. Dick was in his mid-20s, like Mark, but he already had the hard and worldly wise look of an experienced secret agent. Or at least he resembled what Mark thought a secret agent would look like.

"So you already talked to Lucy?" Dick the Welshman said as he poured Mark more gin and tonic.

"Yeah, and she told me her theory about The Antichrist."

"And what do you think?"

"Well, it all sounds kind of whacked out to me."

"That's okay Mark; you don't have to believe her ideas about The Antichrist. I'm not sure I believe it myself—all that supernatural stuff. But what I do believe is that a wad of men, working behind the scenes, are trying to put Nickelay Dubyah into power, him and his New World Order. It's going to be some kind of Anglo-American alliance that covers the U.S., the U.K., most of Eastern Europe, and large parts of Asia, Africa and the Middle East. I'm not sure yet what they are planning. From what I can tell, they already have a deal with the Russian mob to keep the Kremlin on the sidelines, much the same way the Communists knocked Russia out of World War One. But, hey, the Russian mob works cheap. Besides, the Russians are too busy with Chechnya to mess with the N.W.O."

Mark suddenly visualized the wrestler Hulk Hogan smashing a folding chair over the head of the Russian Premier.

"I don't know what you mean. How can these guys control the world?"

"Well, Mark, look at it this way. Every time they get together, things happen. They set agendas, they make long range plans, they control global markets. And worse."

"Worse?"

"They engage in genocide. And no one really even knows it's happening."

"That sounds crazy."

"It's true. These guys make long range plans, and mass murder is just another tool they use to achieve their goals."

"You're talking about criminal activities on a massive level."

"The only difference between murdering one man and murdering a thousand is that the mass murderer has the advantage of the Economy of Scale. Ask any Business major."

"But what could they hope to gain?"

"Back in the early 1970s most world leaders were worried about Revolution. The anti-war movement in America was only one manifestation of a general desire for freedom across the world. And then the unthinkable happened. President Nixon was forced to resign from office. So these world leaders decided that they had to do something drastic. A group of these world leaders got together, led by Dubyah's father, Nickelay the Elder; and they came up with a plan. They financed a special bio-weapons lab set up in a remote part of Africa. They staffed the lab with the best biochemists that the Vatican could find, people who would keep their mouths shut."

"Why? Why would they do such a thing?"

"Look! Here they were on the verge of a world revolution, and the cutting edge of that movement was the sexual revolution. From their point of view, something had to be done—no matter how extreme the consequences—to squash that sex stuff. I mean, you had American Catholics in open rebellion against the Vatican. You had slogans like 'Make love not war' in the United States. You had young people all over the world fucking Authority into oblivion. In order to maintain their power, these world leaders had to act. People nearly stopped believing in The Cold War. Extreme measures were necessary to maintain power. And so they did it."

"Did what?"

"They created a disease, a sexually transmitted disease, and they did it knowing that it would force young people into more 'moderate' behavior."

"You're not serious. They created AIDS in a laboratory in Africa?"

"Yes, even the acronym AIDS was their creation. These letters stand for the name of the bio-weapons team, which translated means 'The Invisible Hand of God.' They meant for this disease to be a killer, just as syphilis was in the 19th century."

"That's crazy!"

"Crazy like a fox. Once the disease was out there, people backed away from revolution, they backed away from sexual experimentation. They resigned themselves to living mediocre lives. They stopped looking for meaning, and instead turned to the churches to find meaning for them. They traded in their real lives for the promise of some future life in the sky."

"But this disease doesn't recognize power. These world leaders, they and their families would be victims of the disease, too."

"But not in the same numbers. You see, they bet that scientists would come up with a cure, or at least a treatment. And they knew that the treatments would be very expensive. They were willing to take a chance, knowing that the wealthy and powerful would have access to the best medical treatment in the world. It was the poor and the helpless who would suffer the most."

"This is just too bizarre to believe. They would condemn millions to a certain death, just to maintain power?"

"Pope Pius XII kept quiet about the deaths of six million Jews, because he hoped Hitler would defeat the Atheistic Communists in Russia."

"That's just a wild accusation."

"It's history. Hitler was a Christian, and he was in good standing with the Vatican right up to the bitter end."

"And you have evidence for all this?"

"It took me a long time to put the pieces together. But, yes, I have the evidence. I also have the name of the scientist who probably led the research team in Africa. You know him, Mark."

"I know him?"

"Yes, his name is Dr. Chumm Rosegarden. You met him in Israel a few weeks ago."

Mark left the meeting with Richard Burton, shaken to his very core as he returned to his hotel. Richard had shown him part of the evidence he had gathered. He even gave Mark the name of the international financier who supported Dr. Rosegarden's research. This was the most surprising name of all. Mark had heard of Jonathan Seagull, but he thought the man was retired. According to Richard, this same Jonathan Seagull had made a fortune in pharmaceuticals, actually several fortunes. Jonathan Seagull had money in anti-depressants, he had money in antibiotics. In fact, he had money in anything that had "anti" in it. It wasn't hard to imagine he had money in The Anti-Christ, too. And he was the money behind Dr. Rosegarden's latest discovery: the Super Fertilizer. Mark had no idea when he'd met Dr. Rosegarden in Israel that his fertilizer research was funded by Seagull. Seagull had even paid for Rosegarden's high-tech wheelchair.

The news from Dick was bad. Really bad. The N.W.O. had reopened the bio-weapons lab in Africa. And god knows what plans the New World Order had.

Mark packed his clothes, flipped open his computer, and checked his messages. But he didn't even have the energy to look at the 35 "Urgent" messages from someone named "I. M. Eighteen." His head was spinning. And all because of Lucy Washington and Dick the Welshman.

Mark couldn't believe it. When he'd met Dr. Rosegarden a few weeks ago, he was impressed by Rosegarden's charm and ready wit. Could Dr. Rosegarden have developed this fertilizer not to help mankind but as a political weapon for Seagull, Dubyah, and the New World Order? It was insane. It was crazy. But maybe it was just crazy enough to be true.

* * *

The phone rang. Ramrod Steel rolled over on his back and reached to grab the phone. His pants were unzipped and his "morning visitor" was already standing at attention, even before he recognized the voice on the other end of the line: Hadshe.

"Ramrod, I'm so glad you're there."

Groggily he answered, "Yeah, I'm here all week, three shows a day."

"I was lonely. I thought I'd give you a call."

"I'm glad you did. I was just lying here on the bed." Suddenly Ramrod's eyes filled with tears and he choked out a gurgling cry.

"What's wrong Rammy?"

He hesitated. Would Hadshe believe him? "It's my wife. She's gone."

"Gone. You mean she left you?"

"Yeah, I guess you could say that. She's gone. And she's not coming back. Ever."

"I'm sorry to hear that. I always thought she must be a very nice woman. At least from what you said about her."

"Yes, she was, and I don't know what to do. I miss her so much already." Ramrod grabbed his wife's dainty underthings and began to wipe the tears from his eyes.

"I wish I could help you."

"Just hearing your voice. It means so much to me. I mean that you would call . . . and that you would ask about me, and how I'm doing. Well, it just means so much."

There was an awkward pause.

"All I have left," Ramrod said, "are her bedclothes . . . and her undies . . . I think. Where did I put them?"

Ramrod looked around, then finally realized that his wife's panties were in his hand. He rolled onto his back and made himself comfortable.

"Hadshe," he said.

"Yes, Rammy"

"What are you wearing?"

Ramrod thought of this call as a first date, sort of. And he was happy that Hadshe quckly got into the spirit of the thing.

"Well, when I got home I slipped out of my flight attendants uniform. You know the new tan uniform I wore today."

"Yes."

"Well I took off the jacket and hung it on a hanger, and I hung it on the back of my closet door. And then I unzipped my tan skirt and stepped out of it, and then I hung it on a skirt hanger."

"Yeah."

"Well, then I unbuttoned my white cotton blouse. One button at a time, because my fingers are so tired from serving drinks all day."

"Yeah, sure, then what?"

"Well, then I sat on the edge of the bed, wearing my black lace bra, and I began to take off my nylons. You know that can be a long, slow process, too."

"Oh yeah, I know it. You have to kinda roll them down."

"I roll them down, one leg at a time. And then I put them on the bed. And then I have to take my bra off. So I slide the straps down, one arm at a time, and then reach around to undo the hooks. And then I can slip off my bra and throw it on the bed, next to my nylons."

"Oh yeah, then what?"

"Then I get my terrycloth robe, the white one, out of my closet. After such a long day, I have to take a shower. So I walk into the bathroom and reach into the shower. I grab the faucet, hard, and twist it so the hot water comes rushing out."

"Ohhh. Yeah! Yeah! Then what?"

"Then I take off my robe and hang it on the back of the door. But I don't close the door. I like to leave it open. And then I put my foot into the stream of water, to test how hot it is. And it's always too, too hot. So I reach in again with my hand and turn the knob back a little bit, just a little twist to cool off the water a little. And then I step into the shower, which has smoky glass walls and a lot of space. And then I take the handle of the shower massage and spray water all over my hot, sweaty body. And I keep it there for a long time, just letting the massage action work its way into my tired, aching muscles. And the water pours over my skin and splashes down over me."

"OHHH YEAH."

There was a brief silence.

"You okay, Rammy?"

"Ah . . . I'm fine."

"Are you sure you don't want me to come over. Maybe I could help you look under the bed for your wife's things?"

"No, I'm okay. I tell you what. I'll call you tomorrow."

Suddenly, Ramrod hung up, leaving a dead silence and then a tone on the other end of the line.

SIX

During the drive home, Cloye Steel had time to think over and over again about what she would tell her Mom and Dad. After all, how do you explain getting expelled from college for "Sacrilege"?

Sitting in the back seat of her Buick, was Jesus. He was just hanging around on his 3x5 wood and barbed-wire crucifix. He was looking a bit guilty, hanging there with blood on his hands. As he stared at her, a song came bursting into Cloye's mind, a variation on the old Christian hymn:

I don't care if it rains or freezes
long as I got my five-foot Jesus
sitting in the back seat of my caaaar . . .

Around her Cloye could see hundreds of other drivers, dodging in and out, all over the highway, and trying to pass each other so that they could arrive at home 45 seconds sooner than they would if they drove at a normal speed. Dozens of them were driving wildly and talking on cell phones at the same time, apparently oblivious to the laws of physics and the dangers of trying to divide attention between driving and talking. For a few seconds Cloye marveled at the miracle of all these hundreds of drivers somehow making it home each day, on a regular basis, without being killed in an enormous pileup. It seemed to her that there was more genuine mystery in this marvel of human skill, than in all the plaster saints and fake blood trails in the history of the Church.

Cloye was still confused about why Professor Wyatt had praised her art project, and then in a strange about face gave it a lowly "honorable mention" in the Art contest. What Cloye didn't realize was that, after thinking about the cross, wrapped in barbed wire, Professor Wyatt suddenly began to suspect that this cross was a political statement. In fact, only a year or so before, a gay man had been murdered in Wyoming and his body tied to a fence post with barbed wire. Was Cloye's art project a political and/or religious statement? Given the turmoil over Cloye's painting of Minnie and the suspicion on campus that Cloye might be a lesbian, Professor Wyatt decided to take the easy way out. After all, over the years several faculty members on campus had wondered about Professor Wyatt and the fact that he wasn't married and didn't even have a steady girlfriend. Might Wyatt, himself, be gay? In fact, like most 20th-century fundamentalist males between the ages of 12 and 42, Professor Wyatt's closest sexual relationship was between himself, a mail order catalog, and a bottle of personal lubricant. Whether his catalog was a Victoria's Secret or an International Male—can be left to the imagination.

As she drove down the highway, Cloye put her fingers to her necklace. It was a charm that Minnie had given to her. Minnie was running a fairly profitable small business from her dorm room, selling charms and love potions to the other coeds.

Minnie's latest venture was taking state commemorative quarters, punching a hole along the top edge, and then adding a leather thong to turn the quarter into a necklace charm. Each state quarter had a different magical power, based on the design. Minnie sold lots of charms made from Georgia quarters. The Georgia quarter had a large peach as its design. Minnie sold this charm, saying, "This will keep you from getting a fat ass."

Minnie had her own, rather unusual ideas of what the various state designs meant. The North Carolina quarter, with its image of the Wright brothers' airplane, inspired Minnie to say, "Buy this one if you plan a trip by airplane; you should get this for your father."

The Maryland quarter, with its tall, narrow capitol building: "Ahh, this one makes your boyfriend strong and virile."

The Tennessee quarter, with its guitar: "This one helps with a music career—even classical music. The Missouri quarter, with a giant arch hanging over the Mississippi: "This keeps your IUD from falling out—good mojo for birth control."

The Kentucky quarter with a horse standing behind a fence: "This one is good to help you find a well-hung boyfriend." The Florida quarter, with a map of Florida: "This one will make your boyfriend impotent if he cheats on you." The Texas quarter with a picture of the Alamo: "This one is good if you want to find a bathroom in a hurry."

Minnie had a good luck charm for every occasion. And sometimes she forgot and sold the same quarter with a completely different magic power. For example, the Arkansas quarter, which had a diamond design, was good for prosperity. But it was sometimes also good for preserving Virginity—at least until the guy promises to marry you. "It works when you put the quarter on the inside of your left knee and hold it in place with your right knee." Minnie sold lots of these charms to coeds who wanted to be "born again virgins." She made enough money just on the Arkansas quarters to pay for all of her books and fees.

When Cloye took the last of her boxes from the dorm room and packed it in the trunk of her Buick, Minnie had kissed her and placed around her neck a Virginia quarter hanging from a leather thong. The picture on the quarter was of a sailing ship landing in Virginia. Minnie said, "This is the kind of ship they used to bring my ancestors to New Orleans. They were slaves. And this charm will protect you so you won't become a slave, too."

Cloye held the Virginia quarter in her clenched fist as she turned off the highway. The exit ramp was crowded with rush hour traffic, and soon she would be home with her family.

* * *

Mark Doody closed his e-mail account and then spent some time on the internet. After losing about $475 at an online casino, Mark went on to look up more information about Nickelay Dubyah.

The online newspapers had several small articles about the fact that Dubyah was running for the office of "Fearless Leader" in his native Texrectumstan. His party's nominating convention had just started, and everyone fully expected Dubyah to be nominated the following night in a nationally televised convention. Soon there would be a national election, and Dubyah was heavily favored to win the election, despite the fact that national polls showed him to be at least 20 percentage points behind the front-runner.

But Dubyah had pulled ahead in more difficult races than this. And, just to make sure, one of Dubyah's aides had bought a Kentucky state quarter charm from an Internet site, and it was being shipped by airmail from Minnie Ball's Magic Charm web site somewhere in Illinois.

Mark went back to his e-mail account and sent a message to his boss at the *Weekly Whirled News*.

"Have to fly to Texrectumstan. Big story."

Mark went online and bought his airline tickets, including an overnight stop in London so he could see Lucy Washington. He also planned to see "The Welshman" one more time and get an update on the activities of The Antichrist. Mark sent e-mails to Lucy, suggesting a hotel where they could get together, and an e-mail message to "Welshman555" suggesting a bar where they could meet a half-hour later. Mark was determined to get on top of this story, stay on top of this story, and ride this story into the ground like a Welsh sow.

Mark had two hours before his flight left, so he went back to the online casino, lost another $245 and then went to the "Willing Hirsute Russian Ladies" website, just in case he could work in a side trip to visit an old girlfriend in Veronish, Russia.

Suddenly his e-mail said "You've got mail" and Mark found a reply from his boss. "What the $%@#*&% are you going to Texrectumstan for? And who is this Lucy Washington who keeps showing up on your expense account?!!!" The e-mail went on at length, speculating on the marital status of Mark's parents when he was born, and suggesting a hot, dark place where Mark should go as soon as possible.

Mark usually ignored his boss's tantrums, and so he signed off his e-mail.

Mark went back to the casino one more time, lost $145, and then managed to win back $168 in a lucky pull of the slots. The screen of his laptop flashed "WINNER" over and over, and the sound card in his laptop played "You're in the Money" over and over again. Mark began dancing, or what he thought was dancing. Several people in the lounge gave Mark funny looks. So Mark danced his "touchdown" dance and said, under his breath, "Hey, at least I'm breaking even , just like my hero, Bill Bennett!" And just like the former Secretary of Education, Mark considered himself a real "player."

The computer piped up again with, "You've got mail." Mark stopped jerking spasmodically. This time it was an email from Mark's father in California. The message said, "Call your father."

"Oh, shit!" Mark said, out loud and a bit louder than he meant to.

SEVEN

An hour later Mark settled himself in the plush first-class seat and waited for the 747 to ascend. He hoped desperately that if he put off calling, just a few minutes more, his father might leave the house on an errand. Mark would be much happier to leave a message on his father's answering machine. That might buy him a few more days before having to return the call.

Mark's father, a prominent entertainment lawyer, had divorced his mother while Mark was still very young. His father then married his secretary, a buxom Hispanic woman, and adopted her two older sons.

Mark's older stepbrothers had made his life a living hell. The boys, both teenagers, had abused Mark on a regular basis. They also threatened to cut off his "chorizo" if he ever told.

Mark soon became a "problem child" and was sent away to a Christian military academy, where he was, once again, abused by the older boys. But Mark was a bright kid and soon figured out ways to avoid trouble—for example, buying a pair of steel-toed boots. Like many of the younger cadets, he was often harassed by the upper classmen. At the Senior Ball, Mark was forced, while dressed as supermodel Kathy Ireland, to participate in a cross-dressing "Beauty Contest."

When traveling, Mark often had time to think back on his life and the steps that led him into journalism. He had no trouble remembering the event that had started him in his journalistic career. As young cadets, Mark and the other freshmen were required "by military tradition" to circle-jerk all the Senior Class Officers under the tables at the pre-graduation breakfast. The following year, as a sophomore, Mark wrote a powerful and compelling expose of this practice for an underground newspaper, *Beyond the Streets & Sheets*. That's how Mark earned his first $50 as a professional writer.

In spite of these challenges, and more, Mark had graduated from the academy and gone on to college, where he majored in journalism

His older brothers were jealous of Mark's success. They had started a promising venture-capital pharmaceutical business, but they were struggling to survive in a dog-eat-dog world, the mean streets of Hollywood and Bel Air.

Mark generally avoided having anything to do with his father and his father's new family. He still occasionally called his mother, but it was often hard to track her down between her apartment in Manhattan and the chateau in Marseilles.

And so it was reluctantly that Mark picked up the phone that was mounted to the seat in front of him, and called his father.

"Hey, Pop, it's me," he said as the answering machine picked up. "I'm on my way to Texrectumstan to do a story on Nickelay Dubyah. He'll probably be picked Man of the Year by *Time* magazine."

Suddenly there was a click.

"What the fuck you callin' here for?" he heard as his step-brother Ricky answered the phone.

"I got an e-mail from Pop. He asked me to call."

"Well, take your candy-ass shit someplace else. He ain't here, and I'm busy."

"Please tell Pop I called—" and the phone went dead. Mark put the receiver back in its niche and ordered a bourbon from the flight attendant, a hirsute brunette who was nice enough to give him a lacy paper napkin with his plastic glass.

* * *

Ramrod Steel went downstairs and fixed himself a large tumbler of whiskey. He settled back in his chair and stared at the liquor and the ice, floating innocently enough in the new Precocious Minutes plastic tumbler his wife Ireme had bought at the local Bibles-R-Us store in the mall in Cherryvale. The plastic tumbler was shaped to reveal the face of a Precocious Minutes Angel; this one was sitting on a cloud and drinking Kool-Aid from a similarly shaped tumbler.

Ramrod's eyes focused briefly on the face, which resembled his lost son Doray, and suddenly he threw the tumbler across the room, where it shattered against the inlaid tiles of his fireplace. Bits of plastic flew in every direction. "At least that cheap plastic shit won't cut anyone," Ramrod said as he padded off to the kitchen to make himself a sandwich.

On the counter he found the Precocious Minutes Bible that Ireme had given Doray for his birthday last year. On the cover was a watercolor sketch by the artist, Frank Slaughter, who had created and trademarked the Precocious Minutes line of Christian figurines. The illustrations inside the Bible were actually the work of Chinese artists who were paid $10 an hour to create the designs.

When they did the Precocious Minutes Bible, the Chinese artists made more than a few mistakes, being unfamiliar with the stories they were illustrating.

The sketch of "Adam and Eve in The Garden" showed both adults, looking like the typical Precocious Minutes children. The sketch showed Eve with a bare waist and a prominent navel—an outie. The Adam also had a navel, and both characters wore clothes made from fig leaves. This picture also had Adam and Eve wearing Nike tennis shoes (probably as part of a product placement deal).

However, the picture of the murder of Abel by his brother Cain (using a samurai sword) was too explicit and had been rejected by the editors.

The sketch of Noah's ark showed a childlike Noah standing next to a ship and smoking a cigarette. The line of animals entering the Ark was well done, but in the background you could see a unicorn at the end of the line. (Noah must have run out of space.)

The sketch of the Tower of Babel was too grim, and several versions had to be commissioned before the artists produced an acceptable image. The illustration showing a plane crashing into the Tower was flatly rejected.

Abraham's sacrifice of Isaac was, also, too bloody; and the Chinese seemed to have confused the sacrifice with a circumcision.

For some reason the sketch of Sodom vs. Gamorrah was rejected, even after the artists offered to include in the sketch, at no extra charge, a giant robotic Godzilla.

The sketch of "Lot licking the Pillar of Salt" was also rejected.

Similarly, Jacob's hot-oil wrestling match with The Angel was rejected.

The weirdness went on and on.

Part of the problem came from the fact that the Chinese artists were given paintings by the "Old Masters" to imitate in creating sketches. But they copied the titles of the paintings, too. So some of the captions in the Precocious Minutes Bible were verbally confusing and seemed to suggest that several famous Italian, French, German and Dutch painters were directly responsible for major Biblical events.

For example, the caption for the sketch of baby Moses floating on the Nile was "Moses Saved from the Waters of the Nile by Orazio Gentileschi."

The sketch of Sodom & Gomorrah was "The Destruction of Sodom by Jean Baptiste Corot."

The miracle of Moses and the rock was "Moses Striking the Rock by Adam van Noort."

The birth of Christ was "Adoration of the Shepherds by Bartolome Esteban Murillo."

The scourging of Christ was "Christ Ridiculed by Hans Holbein the Younger."

Leafing through his son's Bible, Ramrod did not linger long enough to think about the stories, the cheesy artwork or the cheap paper. His real concern was for his daughter Cloye. And when his eyes fell on the sketch which, allegedly, represented "Christ's Raising of Jarius' Daughter by Ilya Efimovich Repin" his head began to swim and he sat down on one of the barstools next to the kitchen counter.

Ramrod picked up the telephone and tried calling Cloye's dorm room, but all he got was Minnie's answering machine message:

"Welcome to Minnie's Charms, Lotions and Notions. If you want to place an order you can go to our website. Or leave a message for me and I'll get back to you, Goddess willing and the creek don't rise."

Ramrod thought he'd dialed the wrong number, but when he dialed it again he got the same bizarre message.

Where was Cloye, and who the hell was this Minnie person?

* * *

Mark was lucky and managed to catch a few hours sleep on the 747 from Chicago. As soon as his plane reached the terminal in London, he ran outside and caught a cab. It was only a few minutes to the hotel, and he hoped desperately that Lucy Washington would still be waiting for him. In his e-mail he asked that she be there at 10 p.m. London time.

The hotel was a shabby old structure that survived mainly because of its nearness to Heathrow airport. The bankers who owned the building were only willing to pay for minor and superficial repairs, leaving the hotel staff to deal with the day-to-day problems of badly stained linens and intermittent hot water.

Mark's cab driver was a Pakistani, and he was constantly muttering to himself about the heavy traffic and the likelihood of getting a tip. His turban bobbed menacingly. Then, suddenly, the driver pointed to the horizon at some strange sort of aircraft passing overhead.

"Look! Look!"

Mark could see the black shape as it moved across the horizon.

"Black helicopters, see! Black helicopters!"

Mark, who had written more than a dozen stories about the infamous Black Helicopters, leaned forward in alarm. What were they doing? Why were they flying now, before it was completely dark? What kind of emergency could send the Black Helicopters out now, at dusk? It was a bad omen.

Mark climbed out of the cab, which smelled vaguely of curry and Old Spice, and entered the front door of the hotel, which smelled of Old Spice and curry. The hotel manager was a Pakistani who glared menacingly toward anyone who came near the front counter. But Mark walked up to him anyway, as there was no other way to get his room key.

"Ah, Mr. Mark," the manager said, as his glare shifted into a smirk, "Miss Lucy has already taken the key and gone up to your room, number 669. I offered her room 666 which is a nicer suite, but she refused it."

Mark nodded, slipped the elderly Pakistani a couple of pound notes, and went to the ancient caged elevator. Taking the steps would have been much faster, but Mark was nearly exhausted from his round trip flight to Chicago.

Lucy met him at the door, wearing a pink silk kimono and not much else. She had made a pitcher of margaritas and had ordered a bowl of mixed fruit from room service.

"Why you back so soon, Honeypot?"

"I got an e-mail from The Welshman. I'm going to be meeting him later tonight."

Mark stripped off his sports jacket, then stripped off his shirt and slacks (pausing only to slip off his penny loafers), and then slipped out of his underwear—a black cotton design covered with happy faces. He jumped onto the bed like a baseball player sliding into home.

Lucy joined him, putting the pitcher of margaritas on the night stand and then rolling onto the bed with a couple of plastic glasses in her hand. It was clear from her movements—like a catfish flopping on a riverbank—that Lucy had already had a few margaritas.

Five minutes later Mark wished he had taken up smoking so that he would have something sexy and "cool" to do in a situation like this.

Lucy rolled over and said, "So what did The Welshman have to say, that got you to fly back here so fast?"

"There's a secret bio-weapons lab. He told me it was open for business again, after being closed for ten years."

"You mean the bio-weapons lab in Africa?"

"Yeah. How did you know about that?"

"I had a dream about it, baby, a baaad dream." She looked toward the window as she slurred, "very, very baaad."

"Do you want to tell me about it? We can talk off the record if you want."

"No, let's just fo'get about it fo' now." Lucy said, dropping her brisk British accent as she slipped into her "North America, Southern States" accent. "Besides, Honey Chile, there's somethin' mo' impo'-tant we hafta to talk about."

"What's that, Miss Lucy?"

"The En' of the World, Honey. It's comin' and it's comin' soon. It's just like the Bible says. God is gonna take his people up in The Rapture, and only the poor sinnahs is gonna be left. And they is gonna hafta fight, an' fight like Hell, agin' The Antichrist."

"I guess I still don't know what The Rapture is all about."

"Whall, it's like this. The Bibles say that two men will be standin' in a field. One man will disappear, in the blink of an eye, and the otha man will be left behind. Except it will go on all over the world. God will come down an' take his chilluns back to Heaven. The only ones left behind are the sinnahs. And that's when The Antichrist is going to come and conquer the earth. He will rule the earth until Jesus Christ, himself, come to destroy the power of The Antichrist."

"So, one day, a whole lot of people are just going to up and disappear?"

Lucy flopped her arms around, like a drunken seagull trying to fly. “That’s right. And I plan to be one of ‘em.”

Wearing nothing but his white socks, Mark got up from the bed, walked over to the window and looked down on the city below them. From the sixth floor, Mark had a God’s eye view of the street.

“You mean it’s like that guy,” pointing to the street, “is going to disappear, but this guy,” pointing to the street vendor, “he’s going to be left behind?”

“Tha’s right,” Lucy said as she reached down and picked up her T-shirt. The shirt had written on the front: “In case of Rapture, this shirt will have no bod.” Lucy pulled the shirt on, over her heavy breasts.

Mark went into the bathroom and turned on the shower. As she heard the water begin to splash down, Lucy picked up Mark’s wallet from the table. She began leafing through his credit cards and cash.

Mark was pressed for time, and so only did a quick rinse off, just to take out the acrid smell of sweat, mixed with Old Spice and curry. As Mark stood under the hot streaming water, he sang, “Lucille, you’re breaking my heart, you’re shaking my confidence, daaaaily” in a voice that could cut glass.

Even though Mark had been out of the room only a few minutes, when he returned Lucy was gone!

There was a smell in the air, like burnt plastic.

Mark walked over to the bed and saw his wallet, lying amid the rumpled sheets. The wallet was partially burned, with melted credit cards and a few pieces of burnt cash. The rest was all gone. Next to the wallet was Lucy’s T-shirt, also badly burnt around the armpits and scorched in several places.

“Holy Crap!” he said. “It’s burnt just like the Holy Shroud of Turin!”

His eyes grew wider as he slowly came to realize what had happened.

“Holy Shit! Lucy was taken up in The Rapture.”

There was nothing left of Lucy, herself, but a great big greasy spot on the bed—evidently the unsanctified remains of a fish ‘n chips dinner—and the burnt shirt. It was like some weird form of teleportation, straight out of *Star Trek*.

With his wallet burned, Mark had to rely on his emergency cash, hidden in a hole in the heel of his shoe. This would be enough money to get him across town tomorrow morning to a safe deposit box, where he kept a phony passport and extra cash. All he could think of was that he had to get out of England as fast as he could, before there was some kind of police investigation.

After struggling to get his shoes on, he fought with his pants and wrestled with his shirt and jacket. He was nearly hysterical by the time he was ready to leave.

Mark took what was left of Lucy's burnt shirt and the wallet, and put them in a plastic trash bag he found in the bathroom. He could get rid of those later. There was no corpse to get rid of, thank goodness—God had provided. Mark thought, "No one knows I saw Lucy. I can say that she was gone when I got to the room."

As he pulled the door closed and locked it, he suddenly remembered that he had to go see Richard Burton. Mark was late already. He knew that if he didn't show, Dick might start looking for him. He didn't want Dick showing up here at the hotel, asking questions.

There was no way around it. He had to go see Dick the Welshman.

EIGHT

Cloye Steel pulled her old 1994 Buick LeSabre into the driveway. The house was quiet, as if no one was at home. But as she got closer to the front door, she heard the sound of Frank Sinatra singing "My Way" in the background.

As she opened the front door, the smell of booze hit her. It was odd for her dad to drink in the house, at least when Doray was around. Usually he went out to the garage to drink anything stronger than a beer. It was clear from the condition of the house that Ramrod Steel had been rambling around most of the day. She could hear him fumbling around upstairs, messing with the CD player in his bedroom.

Cloye went into the kitchen and found her brother's Precocious Minutes Bible sitting on the counter. The Bible was propped open to a spot in Exodus, and the word "Precious" was written in the margin in crayon. Cloye thought, "That boy has watched *Lord of the Rings* one time too many."

She leafed through the pages dealing with the Plagues of Egypt and Moses freeing the Israelites from bondage. It seemed the Egyptians were really into chains and leather, at least that's the way it looked in the movie *The Ten Commandments*.

Cloye always thought of Moses as being kind of like Jimmy Hoffa. Both men were labor organizers and both men were buried in unmarked graves.

Unlike her father, Cloye had sat through many homilies and sermons over the years, not to mention what seemed like endless hours in Sunday School and several Vacation Bible Schools. She was as familiar with the Bible stories as anyone she knew, except maybe the Jehovah's Witness kid in her high school class who had memorized the Bible, backwards and forwards. Cloye lived with the Bible stories most of her life, and she found the behavior of the Jewish Patriarchs to be mostly selfish—when it wasn't vulgar, degenerate, or otherwise depraved.

The story of Lot offering his daughters to a gang to be raped—this was one of her unfavorites. Lucky for the girls, the street gang was more interested in gang banging the (male, of course) angels who happened to be visiting Lot's house.

And there were plenty of other stories illustrating the low moral standards of the early Patriarchs. For them, lying and fraud were laudatory behavior, to be emulated by their many descendants. Having sex, more or less indiscriminately with various wives, slaves, bondwomen, handmaids, daughters, daughters-in-law—this was all perfectly fine with The Lord God Jehovah, himself a tried and true misogynist. Later on, during the Exodus and after, God directed his Chosen People to steal land and massacre the innocent inhabitants, men and women alike. Of course, girls and women who were virgins could be spared and used for the pleasure of God's Own Anointed: the priests of Jehovah. The Israelite men probably went along with this thinking it would keep the priests away from their wives and children. The priests would be too busy molesting their new sex slaves to bother the children of the Chosen People.

Cloye was mystified by her mother's faith. Ireme's devotion to the Catholic Church, and later to her evangelical church, seemed to defy common sense. Ireme's devotion to a God that despised women —it was like a woman living in an abusive relationship. Why join a church that treated women, at best, as second class citizens?

Cloye used to wonder a lot about her mother's obsessive devotion to The Church. Then, when Cloye was a teenager, her grandmother—Ireme's mother—let the story slip. At the end of her life, Grandma was heavily medicated and often repeated stories about the old days. She even dragged out the old scandals for a good airing.

One day, Grandma began talking about the time when Ireme was about ten years old and Father McFeeley took young Ireme on a picnic alone. Father McFeeley's "picnics" were often whispered about in the church. For thirty years the priest had taken young girls on these picnics, usually when the girls were about ten or eleven years old. Many mothers dreaded the day when Father McFeeley would arrive at the door, straw hat in hand, and ask if the daughter was ready to go for a ride to Highland Dam, a remote area of woodlands near Chicago.

On these occasions, the young girl would be dressed in her finest dress, often the same dress she had worn to the previous Easter Mass. The young girl would be presented, wearing her Easter dress and bonnet, and Father McFeeley would take her hand and lead her out to his brown '67 Chevy.

As the girl climbed into the car, adjusting her white dress on the car seat, her mother and older sisters would crowd around the living room window. The women would stare, mill about, and start loud conversations about the weather, or about traffic, or about what they would prepare for the evening supper.

Shortly before dark, Father McFeeley would return in his '67 Chevy, and he would let the young girl out the passenger side door. And always the girl would have a strange look on her face. Anyone who has been to a slaughterhouse and seen a young veal calf hit between the eyes with a hammer would instantly recognize the look in her eyes.

No questions would be asked about the trip. Nothing further would be said. And in time everyone would try to forget what had happened, until the next visit from Father McFeeley. Perhaps he would come for Sunday dinner. Father McFeeley was particularly fond of baked chicken. And what was truly unforgettable about having Father over for a chicken dinner was the look in a young woman's eyes as Father hungrily tore into a chicken leg, a thigh, or a breast.

A few years ago, when Father McFeeley finally retired, Ireme Steel decided that she could now leave the Catholic Church. It was as if some secret agreement she shared with her mother and her sisters and the Virgin Mary, herself had finally expired. Ireme was now released from her promise to The Church and could begin in her own way to find her spiritual answers.

During the last few years, and especially after Cloye turned eighteen, Ireme came to embrace Christianity with the same intense passion that Cloye had in rejecting it.

* * *

Mark Doody found Dick the Welshman waiting for him in an out-of-the-way pub in downtown London. Dick had already eaten a steak supper, knocked back a pint and was starting on a second, all of which would go on Mark's expense account.

An hour late, Mark slipped in the door. He felt like a trapped animal; and when this happened, he didn't want to keep records. Instead, Mark would pay for his meals and the drinks out of his own pocket. Dick didn't mind, as long as Mark paid.

Mark gestured for a pint, his hands trembling, and sat down next to Dick.

"What's wrong with you, mate?" Dick said in his fake Cockney accent. Dick usually slipped into a fake accent whenever he sensed trouble.

"She's gone!"

"She's gone? Who's gone?"

"Lucy. Lucy Washington. She met me in my hotel room and then she just disappeared."

"You mean disappeared like 'left' or disappeared like 'vanished'?"

"I mean disappeared like in a puff of smoke and the smell of burnt plastic—that kind of disappeared!"

"Oh, never seen that one afore. She's good at disappearin' that Lucy is. She disappeared once with me pants, and me wallet still in the back pocket."

"This is different. I think. I think Lucy was taken up in The Rapture!"

"What! Don't be daft."

"It's true. I saw it myself. One minute she was sitting there on the bed. The next minute she's gone. All that was left was my wallet and her shirt. Here, I'll show you."

Mark produced the plastic bag, and Dick carefully examined the charred edges of the wallet, the melted credit cards and the singed bits of cash. Dick started to pull the shirt out of the bag, too, but the smell of Old Spice, curry, and burnt fish 'n chips was so strong that he quickly shoved the shirt back into the bag and sealed it.

"What do you think?" Mark said, a tremble in his voice.

"Well, my first guess would be the Zenon Death Ray."

"The what?"

"The Zenon Death Ray. You remember. The French government was working on a particle beam weapon. It's supposed to be powerful enough to vaporize a water buffalo in eight seconds. But it only affects organic matter."

"I don't know. I still think it was The Rapture."

"Well, what about spontaneous human combustion? It's supposed to leave a burnt smell."

"No. I don't think so."

"Alien abduction?"

"Maybe. Well, no I don't think so."

"Just out of curiosity. How much cash was in this wallet?"

"Almost two thousand dollars."

"Why aren't there more ashes then? Two thousand dollars, even in hundred dollar bills, would leave a lot of ash, wouldn't it?"

"I guess so."

Dick took a small knife out of his pocket and picked up the melted credit cards. He pried apart the top two cards in the stack. The top card was Mark's Sears charge card, but the plastic card just under it was a British gas card with the name "Lucy Washington" embossed in white letters.

"Look at that. Lucy conned you. She melted her own credit cards, with two of yours on the top and bottom. Then she stole your cash and burnt up the small bills. She probably scorched her shirt, too, just to fool you."

"You mean this was just a trick?!"

"Yeah, you ought to know better'n t' leave large sums of cash layin' around with Lucy. Didn't you know she was tryin' to put together enough cash to move back to Liberia and open her own church? She's gonna call it 'The Church of the Immaculate Hand Job' or something like that. Man! You've been had."

"Then . . . you mean Lucy's not dead?"

"No, you idiot, she's probably down right now in Whitechapel selling your platinum credit cards to some gang. By this time tomorrow she'll probably be on a slow boat to Liberia."

"Thank God!"

"What?"

"Thank God. For a minute there I was afraid I'd have to leave the country to avoid a police investigation."

"Don't be daft; the police don't start an investigation every time Lucy decides to fade into the background. I'd guess your two grand probably put her over the top.She's headed back to Africa."

"Well, I guess this means I can fly to Texrectumstan tomorrow and do that story on Nickelay Dubyah."

"Shuuush," Dick whispered, "Keep your voice down. Don't say his name out loud. He has agents everywhere. Didn't you see the Black Helicopters?"

"Well, now that you mention it, I did see some Black Helicopters fly over the city earlier today."

"And do you know where they're going""

"No, I don't."

"Those Black Copters are flying to Texrectumstan. They are going to monitor the elections there. The UN wants to make sure that You Know Who gets elected, no matter what. They can't stand it when some local character gets into power. Look how upset they got when Jimmy Carter got elected. And Boris Yeltsen, don't ask! It just drives them nuts."

"So, do you have any idea how they plan to fix the election?"

"Sure, the government of Texrectumstan just borrowed thirty million dollars to convert their paper ballot system to a touch-screen computer system."

"So?"

"So? Do you know how many guys it takes to fix an election run by computers?"

"No."

"One. It just takes one computer programmer."

"Oh. . . . And how do you know that Dubyah is going to fix the election?"

"Who do you think owns the company that manufactures the voting machines?"

"Uhhh, I don't know."

"He's an international financier named Jonathan Seagull. He's the same man who's been secretly promoting Nickelay Dubyah for years."

NINE

Ramrod Steel heard the refrigerator door open, and in that moment he realized that his most dearly beloved (and only) daughter, Cloye was in the house. Joy welled up in Ramrod's heart as he realized that, although he had lost his only wife and only son, he still had his only daughter who was left behind on earth, the same way he was.

Ramrod dropped the Best of Sinatra CD, where it fell into a pile with his Eric Clapton CD and his Best of John Denver CD. He had played Clapton's "Angel" song over and over again, followed by Elton John's "Candle" song and finally by Joan Jett's "I hate myself for loving you." Then he put the Sinatra CD in the player, hoping that, since Sinatra was in Heaven, too, he could keep Ireme company until Ramrod got there. He even went into Cloye's room to look through her CDs, but all he found was Jimi Hendrix, Queen, 2pac Shakur, Sam Kinison and Bill Hicks CDs. He was sure there was no one in that group that Ireme would want to hang out with, now that she had crossed over to the next world. In fact, she had on more than one occasion called Cloye's music "satanically inspired." Ireme insisted that Cloye buy only Christian Rock or "sanitized" Pop Music CDs from Wal-Mart.

Ramrod found his wife's Bible, or at least one of the four or five Bibles that she used, sitting on the dresser next to her costume jewelry. He said to himself, "I guess there's no time like the present. I've got to confront Cloye over her lack of faith."

Meanwhile, Cloye was making herself a baloney and catsup sandwich and pouring a glass of 2% milk. She wondered where her mother was. By now, Doray should be home from church school, too, unless he had a late practice with the Fighting Squirrels pep squad.

Ramrod moved sluggishly down the stairs. He saw Cloye in the kitchen.

"Hi, honey."

"Hi, Dad."

Ramrod tried to ease into the conversation.

"Do you remember back when you were sixteen, and your pet cat Squeekers ran under a car and was killed?"

"Yeah, sure."

"And your mother told you that Squeekers had gone to Heaven."

"Yeah. So?"

"And you said it didn't matter 'cause Squeekers was gone. And it didn't matter where."

"I remember. What are you getting to?"

"Your mother and your brother. They're gone."

"Gone where?"

This was the hard part.

"Gone to Heaven."

Cloye stared at her father and saw the sad expression on his face. For a second she thought her father meant "Heaven" as a euphemism for IHOP, the International House of Pancakes. But from her father's expression, she knew this was wrong.

"They've gone to Heaven? You mean Heaven, the eternal place of peace, *Heaven*?"

"Yes, that's right, honey. Your mother and brother have gone to Heaven. Maybe, if we're lucky, we can join them there, too."

For a second Cloye wondered if her father had finally snapped from listening to her mother's endless chatter about God, and Heaven, and Christ, and the Angels, and the Bible, and the Holy Spirit, etc., etc., etc., on and on, *ad infinitum*. An image popped into her mind of her father strangling his wife and his sexually ambiguous son and burying them both in the back yard.

But her father was really too boring to have done such a thing. He was not at all like that lunatic killer, the hayseed in the movie *Frailty*. Her Philosophy professor at Bible college had shown this film in his New Testament classes as an example of what would happen in The Last Days. The professor had also shown them a new documentary, featuring Dr. Harold Cox, about The Tribulation. In the film Dr. Cox showed them a map of the United States and how every major serial killer in the country had been born in a circular area between Des Moines on the western edge and the eastern border of Ohio. This "Circle of Evil" ran up to the Canadian border on the north and went south all the way to St. Louis. Based on this map, Dr. Cox proclaimed that Hammond, Indiana—at the "center" of the circle—was "The Spiritual Scrotum of Satan" and that the future Antichrist would probably be born there.

It was obvious to Cloye, though, that her father, Ramrod Steel, was just too unimaginative to be a murderer, much less a first-class serial killer. She must have misunderstood what he said.

"Dad. Where, exactly, are Mom and Doray?"

"In Heaven, honey. I just told you that."

"You mean they're dead?"

"Well, not exactly dead. They were taken up to Heaven, by God."

"Okay. And why did God take them to Heaven?"

"Well, at church you've heard Reverend Bobby's sermons about The Rapture."

"Yes, I remember him saying something about that."

"Well, it's like this. Early this morning we had The Rapture. God came down and took all the people who believe in Him to Heaven. The only people left behind, the only people left on earth, are the people like you and me. We were left behind because God did not recognize us as His people."

"I thought His people were the Jews."

"Oh, I don't think so, honey. I'm sure Reverend Bobby would have said something about that. No, it's only the Christians, the True Christians, who were taken away to Heaven."

"Okay, and how do you know that Mom and Doray were taken to Heaven?"

"There's no other explanation for it. They've disappeared. All that's left behind are their clothes. And it's happening all over the world. People are disappearing, just like it says in the Bible."

"I don't remember hearing anything about it on the radio."

"Well, I don't think it's happening all at once. God is coming down and picking up people, one person at a time."

"I find that hard to believe."

"Just look at this!" Ramrod held up the milk carton with a picture of a missing ten-year-old boy. "And don't you watch *Unsolved Mysteries* on TV. They always have people who have disappeared, never to be seen again."

"I guess . . . but . . ."

"And all those people who claim to be taken by aliens. Maybe they were taken to Heaven by mistake and then God put them back."

"And the Angels gave them anal probes?"

"Well . . . maybe not. But there are still hundreds, maybe thousands of people who disappear every day. Maybe they are being taken up to Heaven."

"Okay, Dad, now you're starting to worry me. So you're saying that Mom and Doray are gone. They've been gone all day. And they haven't called or anything?"

"That's right, honey. They're gone. And they're never coming back."

Cloye rolled this over in her mind for a few minutes, and then realized that she could now search for her sports bras and underwear in Doray's room, which was the only logical place they could have disappeared to.

* * *

Mark drank a dark stout while Dick the Welshman helped himself to a large bowl of chili, Texas style. This was one of the few vices Dick had picked up in America, during his stint as an aerial photographer for *Weekly Whirled News*.

Mark and Dick had become very good friends, in spite of Dick's habit of picking his nose and lifting his leg to fart. Dick also had a selection of "quaint" expressions he had picked up in Australia, including "Well, fuck me with a spoon," "Show me the money," and "Don't tell me she's your wife! Really. You're shittin' me aren't you? You're a lucky man. Just look at the ass on her. Nice rack, too." Dick's bosses at WWN seriously thought about firing Dick or sending him back to London, or perhaps just transferring him to their Houston office.

"So, what can you tell me about the bio-weapons lab in Africa?"

"Not much," Dick said, "only that a lot of Black Helicopters have been seen flying around the old bio-weapons site, and no one can get near it now. Not even the locals are allowed into the area. The government claims the area is closed to protect endangered species, but there's nothing around there except for some stupid, flea-bitten mountain gorillas. And who cares about them, anyway?"

"It's not much to go on."

"There's more than that. I've put together a list of deadly contagious diseases. Viable samples of these diseases have mysteriously disappeared from major research laboratories all over Europe. They include every respiratory disease known to man. Everything from the pneumonic plague to the 1918 influenza strain that wiped out millions of people. Someone is collecting samples of antibiotic-resistant strains of common diseases, even whooping cough, and sending them in frozen nitrogen containers to Africa."

"But why would they want to experiment with that stuff?"

"I don't know. But it's all tied in with Nickelay Dubyah and Jonathan Seagull. They've got something sinister in mind."

"Maybe Seagull plans to create some monster disease, along with a cure. Then he could let the disease loose and make a fortune peddling the drugs to cure it."

"It's possible," Dick said, "Or maybe it's even more horrible than that."

"What do you mean?"

"Just think. Nickelay Dubyah is about to become the leader of Texrectumstan, a country with very serious economic problems. The number of elderly people is growing, but the younger people are leaving the country, emigrating to work in the oil fields in Kuwait."

"So what. Lots of countries have aging populations."

"It's not only that. The government has to pay enormous amounts of money for health care for the elderly. And instead of having the courtesy to die at fifty-five or sixty like they used to, these old people are living into their seventies and eighties."

"So?"

"So what if Seagull's lab creates a disease that kills old people and people with chronic illnesses like diabetes, but does little harm to healthy younger people and children? Pretty soon, as thousands of old people get sick and die off, the economic picture in Texrectumstan gets a lot better. No more old people to support, only young people who are able to work and be productive citizens."

"That sounds wild."

"But it could work, especially if the disease was designed to hit people hardest who live in unsanitary conditions. A disease like that could wipe out half the elderly people in Africa, not to mention what it would do in India and Asia."

"You're talking about a disease that is designed to wipe out the poor and the elderly."

"That's right."

"But that would be genocide on a massive scale. It would make the Holocaust pale by comparison." Mark paused for a moment, his eyebrows twitching. "Have you told anyone else about this?"

"Only you," Dick said, "and a biologist from Yale. But he's an old friend of mine, and I'm sure he won't say anything. Mark looked skeptical, but Dick seemed pretty certain.

Mark decided to catch the first plane to Texrectumstan and find out what was really going on. While Dick finished slurping down his chili, Mark toyed with the idea of catching a red eye.

As they left the pub, Dick stopped at the door and reached inside his shirt. He pulled out a green and white charm tied to a leather thong. "Lucy Washington gave me this a few weeks ago. It's a charm dedicated to the Angel Nichbadiel who grants the spiritual gift of Discernment to anyone who wears it."

"Nichbadiel? I've never heard of him."

"Oh, he's one of the angels in Heaven who guard The Gates of the South Wind."

Mark took the paper charm in his hand. It appeared to be a dollar bill, folded into a triangle, with the image of the pyramid and the "All-seeing Eye" as the central design.

"Wild!" Mark said, "I wish I had one."

Dick grabbed the charm back from Mark and let it fall to his chest. Mark felt that in those few moments the image of the pyramid seemed to actually glow in the darkness, making it look like Dick's chest hairs had caught fire.

"You need a ride back to your hotel?" Dick said.

"No . . . no, that's okay. I can get a cab."

Dick shrugged his shoulders and walked toward his convertible. Mark suddenly remembered that he had forgotten to tip the waitress. He went back into the pub for a second and returned just in time to glance at Dick's antique Sunbeam convertible, as it exploded.

Mark was knocked to the ground by the force of the blast. The whole parking lot was lit up by the bright blue fireball from the blast. He was stunned, but Mark soon pulled himself to his feet and watched as flames belched out of the frame of the shattered Sunbeam. Dick the Welshman was gone, vaporized by the explosion.

Mark looked up at the scattering of sparks and burning ash, and he saw the Charm of Nichbadiel fall from the sky and land at his feet. Mark picked it up.

"I knew eating all that Texas chili would catch up with him someday," Mark said as he waved down a cab. Mark had seen men die in battle before, or at least he had seen men die in front of a camera only a few miles away. But this was somehow different. Dick the Welshman was the closest thing he had to a friend, unless you counted the guys he played ball with at the Y. But here Dick was, dead, blown to tiny charred bits in front of his eyes. How would anyone react to that? What Would Jesus Do? How would *He* react? More important, what would Mark do, now that he was the only person left who could possibly oppose the power of The Antichrist.

But in those moments, standing in the drizzle and waiting for a cab to stop, Mark began to wonder if it really was just a bizarre accident. Could there have been a bomb in Dick's car?

Still in shock from this close call with Death, Mark suppressed his urge to flee. In one night he had lost Lucy Washington, the best Christian escort he had ever met. And he had lost his best friend, Dick the Welshman. But he still had to catch the next flight to Texrectumstan—and as soon as possible. Only there could he find the answers that he so desperately needed.

TEN

The next morning Ramrod Steel decided to drive over to Ireme's new church, The Mt. Saint Mary Divine Observance of God's Grace—Immense, Eternal, Supernatural Through Imminent Life—Evangelical Church, or the Mt. Saint Mary D.O.G.G.I.E.S.T.I.L.E. Church, for short.

Ramrod slept through several phone messages from Hadshe Dunhim that morning, much the same way he'd slept through the Reverend Bobby Black's sermons each Sunday. The most recent call woke him from a dream where Hadshe was an angel floating over his bed. Her honey blonde hair hung down in golden streams, just like in the fairy story of Rapunzel. Ramrod was entranced as her beautiful and delicate hand lowered itself from the heavens and then slapped him across the face.

Ramrod's eyes opened, and he vaguely recognized Hadshe's voice, just as she finished recording a message on his answering machine. The answering machine flashed its little red buttons in a provocative way, but somehow Ramrod found the inner fortitude to resist picking up the phone and calling Hadshe. It was just too early in the morning for Ramrod to think through all the steps necessary to call Hadshe, try to convince her to meet him at a nearby motel, and then go on to Mt. Saint Mary's Church to visit Ireme's old pastor.

Ramrod didn't bother to try to wake Cloye. He was glad he didn't have to deal with her unrelenting skepticism again this morning. She probably didn't really want to go to church with him anyway, even though she had offered to go.

With great effort, he struggled through programming the Mr. Coffee and resetting the clock. A mysterious power outage during the night had scrambled the time on the clock so that it flashed (12:00) over and over again. Ramrod wondered if this was a sign from God, or if maybe a worker at the power plant had been taken up in The Rapture, causing the power outage.

"The ways of God are truly mysterious," he said to no one in particular.

Ramrod put on his best suit, and it was a real challenge to stop himself from putting on his pilot's cap, too. The End of the World would be chaotic, and Ramrod wanted to invest himself with all the authority he could find.

The drive to church gave him time to think. Maybe, there would be someone at the church on a Wednesday afternoon. It seemed to Ramrod that they always had some service or other, or some meeting or class or something on Wednesdays. Ramrod had two or three friends who went to AA meetings at Mt. Saint Mary. Thanks to new federal government regulations and grants from the Faith-Based Charities program, the Mt. Saint Mary Church was generously reimbursed for hosting AA meetings—not to mention Gamblers Anonymous, Narcotics Anonymous, and Sex Addicts Anonymous meetings. And, of course, there were the Prostate Cancer Survivors Group, the Christian Singles group, the Divorced Christians Support Group, the Christian-to-Christian Counseling group. And that's not even including the Christian Elementary School, the Christian Middle School, and the Mt. Saint Mary Christian High School—all of which were generously funded by a new Illinois school voucher program.

There was barely room left over in the basement for the "Let Your Babies Live" Unwed Moms Counseling Group, which had a brand new $48,000 ultrasound machine provided by a federal grant.

Turning into the parking lot, Ramrod was surprised to see so many cars there. He drove slowly past the executive parking lot, watching for the yellow "Ass. Pastor" parking spot, and saw Rev. Bobby Black's new cream-colored Lincoln Continental parked in its usual space. Ramrod wanted to talk to a young minister, someone like Bobby Black, and not to the older Rev. Dr. Bill Eous, who was the Senior Pastor.

Most people driving past Mt. Saint Mary Evangelical Church got the false impression, based on the fabricated steel and concrete block construction, that Mt. Saint Mary Evangelical Church was just another warehouse. In fact, this was God's warehouse and factory, where God's work was done 24/7, usually in cramped working conditions at sub-minimum wage. Thanks to "The Separation of Church and State," which Rev. Black preached against at every opportunity, the church could ignore fire codes, safety codes, sales taxes, property taxes, equal opportunity employment laws, and dozens of other laws and codes that would otherwise make so much trouble for people simply trying to do "God's work."

Ramrod entered the front door, admiring the colored glass in the windows and the fake brickwork. No expense had been spared in preparing God's House. Even the pews were the best that money could buy, mainly because one of the church members owned a carpentry shop and provided the pews for only the cost of materials.

A Bible study group was meeting in the new Main Chapel, and the two annex chapels were being used by the Christian Singles and the Sex Addicts. The old chapel, which faced the street behind, was being used as a practice room by a Christian Rock 'n Roll group, called Our Daily Bread. The music group was funded as an Illinois state after-school program with grant money funneled through the Mt. Saint Mary Christian High School.

As Ramrod entered the new Main Chapel, he saw Reverend Black wave to him. As soon as Rev. Bobby spotted Ramrod, he had handed off the Bible study class to one of the church elders and rushed back to grab Ramrod's hand and shake it ferociously, like a tiger worrying a lamb chop. Rev. Black had an infallible sense for recognizing people with a good cash flow, and Ireme Steel's track record for giving cash donations made Captain and Mrs. Ramrod Steel two of Bobby's favorite parishioners.

"Hello, Captain Steel. Didn't expect to see you here today." Bobby checked the date on his Rolex. "It's not Sunday, is it?"

"No . . . no, Reverend."

"Call me Bobby, just plain ole Bobby. What can I do for you today?"

Reverend Bobby Black was worried and doing his best to hide it. Gossip and rumors were already spreading about how the Senior Pastor, Reverend Bill Eous, had disappeared, along with a large sum of cash and a church secretary. And Captain Steel had a very concerned look on his face.

"Bobby, it's a very sensitive issue. Is there somewhere we could talk?"

"Sure, sure," Bobby said, as he led Ramrod back to his office.

The new faux silk rug and solid walnut-veneer desk gave Reverend Black's office a very distinctive and professional look. Bobby sat down in his leather chair and motioned Ramrod to the worn, but comfortable, chair in front of the desk.

"So, now what can I do for you?"

"My wife, Ireme. She's missing."

The hair stood up on the back of Bobby's neck. Could Reverend Bill have absconded with a church secretary and a female parishioner? It was just too horrible to imagine.

"Missing," Bobby fumbled with the executive pen set on his desk. "Missing how?"

"She just disappeared, and our son Doray is gone, too."

Suddenly sirens and bells went off in Rev. Bobby's head. Not a kid, too!

"Well . . ." Bobby said, buying for time, "What do you think happened to them?"

"I believe . . . I believe they were taken up . . . in . . . The Rapture."

Bobby felt the wind go out of him, like a punch in the gut. This was something he hadn't imagined, hadn't planned for. Clearly Ramrod Steel believed that his wife and son were taken up in The Rapture! Bobby struggled to maintain a straight face. And at the same time millions of neurons were firing in his brain as an idea came to mind. He suddenly remembered the advice of Saint … Saint … Saint

Somebody, who said, "Be as wise as the Serpent and as gentle as the Dove."

"Yes," Bobby said, "Yes, Captain Steel, I think you're right."

* * *

Cloye Steel woke up that morning, grateful to be back in her own bed. She hadn't had the heart to tell her father that she had been expelled from college for "Gross Blasphemy." But she was glad not to have to deal anymore with the gang of loonies who ran the school, not to mention the slutty Christian sorority girls and the horny Christian fraternity boys.

During her youth, spent in various Catholic schools, Cloye had heard plenty of disturbing stories about the "secrets" of the cloister. These stories and the lascivious nature of the Protestant "Greeks" were enough to convince Cloye that most Christians—both Catholic and Protestant—were mainly over sexed and compulsive fornicators, people who found no meaning in life except by struggling (and it was a losing struggle) with various compulsions, including sex, alcohol, drugs, porn, and gambling. They were all so obsessed with "Sin" that they were unable to enjoy life in any normal, healthy way, much less think outside the box of their own sado-masochistic fantasies of Heaven and Hell.

Cloye learned from her Philosophy professor that the followers of Islam were equally obsessed with sex. The Islamic terrorists who crashed into the World Trade Center had all been promised that, dying as Martyrs of Allah, they would enjoy the company of twenty virgins when they reached Heaven. Or was it forty virgins?

Was this the main difference between Islam and Christianity? The Islamic mullah looks forward to an afterlife in the Islamic Heaven, where he will have sex with twenty willing virgins, while the Christian Heaven was full of sexless eunuchs with wings and halos, all singing "Holy, Holy, Holy" day and night, 24/7.

* * *

On the other hand, across town the Reverend Bobby Black had a very different idea of what Heaven was like. Rev. Bobby's idea of Heaven was a long weekend in a sleazy downtown hotel with cocaine, booze and twenty crack whores, half of them wearing strap-ons.

Bobby Black looked Ramrod in the eye, and said, "Captain Steel, I plan to make an announcement at a special service tonight, but since you're here now, and you already suspect what has happened, I might as well go ahead and tell you. The Rapture has come. Our own beloved Reverend Doctor Bill Eous has disappeared, called to Heaven by God. He was sitting here, with me in this office, when suddenly, poof! He was gone. Even his clothes were gone. Not only that, but several other members of our church have disappeared in the same way your wife and son did. And one of our church secretaries. It's a very sad situation for all of us."

"You don't know how happy I am, Bobby, to hear this. For a while I thought I was losing my mind."

"No, no, Captain Steel. You're quite sane."

"Thank God!"

"Yes, we should all thank God."

"But, Reverend Bobby, what did we do wrong? Why were we left behind?"

"I guess most of us just didn't measure up. God must have looked into our hearts and seen the secret sins that live there. And I am probably one of the worst offenders.

"Did I tell you that I have struggled, day in and day out for the last twenty years with the demon of cigarette smoking? It's a horrible, horrible addiction, and I pray to God every day to help free me from its Satanic influence. But even with God's help I wasn't strong enough. So you can see why God left me behind."

Tears began to form in his eyes. "Can you imagine what it's like to spend ten years of your life preaching God's Word, and then to be left behind like this? You can't imagine how difficult this is for me."

"Yeah, I guess that's a tough one all right."

"But I have made a decision in my life. I will do better. I will try harder. I'm going to work, day and night, to make Mt. Saint Mary Evangelical Church the biggest and best church in Chicago, or my name isn't Reverend Robert Black, ABD."

"Is . . . is there anything I can do Reverend Bobby?"

"For now you can pray for me, pray for this church and all of us. We will need strength in these troubled times."

"Yes, of course."

"Soon I'll call on you to help rebuild this church, but in the meantime you can talk to people in the congregation. Testify to them. Testify to the miracle that has happened. They will need all the help we can give them."

"Yep, I'll be glad to."

"And tonight at 8:00 p.m. I'm going to have a special service and show one of the videotapes that Reverend Bill made for us. It describes The End Times and how we will have to deal with the coming of The Antichrist."

"Great, thanks, you can't imagine what this means to me Reverend Bobby."

"It means a great deal to me too, Mr. Steel. So I'll see you here tonight?"

"Absolutely!"

"Good, then tonight we will hear Doctor Eous' message, via the miracle of video, and learn how to survive the coming battle with The Antichrist." Rev. Bobby smiled and put his hands together, as if in prayer. In some way Bobby felt that Ramrod's strange delusion was, indeed, an answered prayer.

ELEVEN

That evening, Mark found his way to the airport to catch the last flight to Texrectumstan. Everything was going well, right up to the point of passing through customs. Then, inexplicably, a customs official called Mark's name and directed him to a small office. Mark felt a chill as the official frowned at him and pointed to a doorway. At first Mark considered dropping his suitcase and running. But instead he went down the hall and entered the office.

"Mark Doody?" the official said.

"Yes."

Mark faced a short, middle-aged civil servant, nondescript in appearance except for a birthmark on his forehead. The official shuffled through the papers in front of him. Several minutes passed, so Mark cleared his throat.

"What?" the official said.

"I have a plane to catch. Is there some way we can hurry up this process?"

"Certainly, certainly Mr. Doody. But this is not a customs investigation."

"No?"

"No. I am investigating the murder of Mr. Richard Burton."

"The actor?"

"Don't play dumb, Mr. Doody. We know you were with Mr. Burton tonight. You were there when his car exploded, weren't you?"

"Wasn't that an accident?"

"An accident. Don't be ridiculous. There was a bomb under the seat of Mr. Burton's car. When Mr. Burton sat down it armed the bomb. Then he must have shifted in his seat and triggered the explosion."

"Oh."

"Not only that, but there seems to be some question about a female escort named Lucy Washington. Evidently you were the last person to see her, also this evening."

"Actually, I didn't see her. She was supposed to meet me at the hotel, but she left before I got there."

"She left before you got there? That doesn't sound like Lucy, does it?"

"I don't know. I really don't know her that well."

"You don't? That's funny. We found that she charged a rather large sum of money against your bank cards last night—a rather considerable sum."

"So?"

"So perhaps that money was payment for a 'hit' on Mr. Burton."

"Good grief, do people really use credit cards to pay for assassinations?"

"I don't know, Mark, perhaps you could tell me."

"Look, I didn't have anything to do with Lucy disappearing, and I don't know anything about anyone trying to kill Dick Burton."

The official shifted in his chair, then looked angry; a tic in his cheek muscles worked itself into a rhythmic throb.

"Why did you say that? Why did you say 'tried to kill Mr. Burton'?"

"I don't know. What difference does it make?"

"Do you wish to offer any explanation at all for your activities earlier tonight?"

"I mean. It was . . . The Rapture."

"The what?"

"The Rapture, you know. The End of the World. It's just like in the Book of Revelations. The true Christians disappear and the rest of us are left behind."

"So it's your assertion that Mr. Burton and Ms. Washington were carried away to Heaven as part of some supernatural phenomenon."

"Yes . . . No . . . I mean . . . it could have happened that way."

"Perhaps, Mr. Doody, you might wish to seek the help of a solicitor."

"Am I being charged with a crime?"

"Perhaps. And where are you planning to fly to tonight?"

"I have to go to Texrectumstan. I have an interview with Nickelay Dubyah."

The official's face went white, while the birthmark on his forehead flushed red. The telephone in front of him rang, just once, and he picked up the receiver.

"Yes. Yes, of course."

The official put the phone down.

"Well, Mr. Doody, it seems that we've made an unfortunate mistake. You are free to go."

Mark practically leapt out of his chair and ran from the room. He didn't stop until he was on the 747 and safely planted in his first class seat.

* * *

Ramrod Steel left his meeting with Rev. Bobby Black, feeling spiritually renewed and energized. It was all true. Ramrod was flush with the feeling of success. He had been vindicated. Reverend Bobby Black had confirmed what Ramrod had suspected all along: Ireme and Doray had been taken up to Heaven as part of The Rapture. And tonight Rev. Black was going to announce this fact to the world.

As soon as Ramrod left the church, Reverend Bobby began going through the church's collection of tapes made by Reverend Bill. There were hundreds of tapes, all made for shut-in parishioners. There had to be a taped lecture on The Rapture that Bobby could use to "prove" that Rev. Bill (and the church secretary) had been taken up bodily to Heaven. It would be a little harder to explain what happened to the $375,000 that had disappeared at about the same time Reverend Bill did. But Bobby was determined to take hold of Mt. Saint Mary Evangelical Church and milk it like a rented Holstein.

* * *

Meanwhile, Cloye Steel had contacted the police and told them that her mother and brother were missing. The policeman told her to come down to the station and fill out a report. From the tone of his voice, Cloye was sure that the police would do little or nothing to find them. This was (in their view) probably just another marital dispute that had gone bad.

Cloye struggled with her emotions. She found her mother's address book and decided to start calling. It took hours, but Cloye called everyone in the book. Then, mentally and emotionally exhausted, after explaining over and over again that her mother had disappeared, Cloye forced herself to search the house for clues.

Cloye was going through her mother's things, trying to figure out what had really happened to Ireme and Doray. As best she could tell, they had left all their stuff behind, except for her mother's cheap costume jewelry and a few clothes. Doray's room was neat and tidy, so Cloye had no way of telling what was missing. But she had to figure out some way to convince her father that Ireme and Doray were still here on earth, somewhere. But how?

Cloye didn't realize it, but Ireme and Doray had rented a rundown apartment on the outskirts of Branson, Missouri. Ireme had applied for a job working at Precocious Minutes Theme Park—a Christian, family-oriented business. Ireme told them she was recently widowed (a little white lie she was sure God would forgive) and that her husband had died in a plane crash. All she had left was her son Doray and enough cash to survive for a few weeks. Ireme was so insistent, and so supplicant and prayerful in the way she asked, that the manager of PMTP hired her immediately and set her up cooking the buffalo wings at 7th Heaven Bar-B-Qued Angelic Wings in the food court.

Ireme had no idea, of course, what was going on back in Chicago, where Rev. Bobby Black was about to use her strange disappearance as the basis for his claim that the Reverend Dr. Bill Eous, Ireme and Doray Steel, and a church secretary had all vanished in The Rapture.

* * *

At the service on Wednesday night, Reverend Bobby Black stood in front of the congregation. He had been planning to give the standard "Do not lay hands on God's anointed" sermon (based on Psalm 105:15), which was normally used when a minister has been caught in a scandal. But the visit from Ramrod Steel had changed all that. Bobby was going to pull the proverbial fat out of the fire, using The Rapture to explain how Reverend Bill and the church secretary had disappeared.

Reverend Bobby was not standing at the podium, where the congregation was so used to seeing the Right Reverend Dr. Bill Eous. Bobby stood over to the left. Standing in front of the podium was a big-screen television and a DVD player.

Reverend Bobby had a natural stage presence, and he knew that leaving the podium empty would give just the right message to the congregation. He didn't want to be seen as grabbing at Reverend Bill's job. Today the recorded message from Reverend Bill was the star of the show. Bobby's time would come, soon enough.

As the choir dragged out the last few words of "We Shall Gather at the River," Reverend Bobby began his message:

"Friends, Brothers and Sisters in Christ, today is a happy day—a happy, happy day. We can rejoice in the Lord, Our God, for the gifts he has bestowed upon us. We should take pride in this day. And you know why? Because God has given us a great gift. God has given us a gift, and we can make great things happen!

"Brothers and Sisters, we have been given a gift from God. It is a gift from God. And do you know what it is? The leader of our flock, our Good Shepherd, the Reverend Doctor Bill Eous, has been taken from us.

"No, he is not dead. Reverend Bill has been taken up to Heaven … in THE RAPTURE! That's right, Reverend Bill was carried away in The Rapture. And today we are here as witnesses to this great miracle that God has done.

"I see a few of you sittin' there with open mouths and tongues a waggin', but hear me out. We are the witnesses of a great miracle. Our

Good Shepherd, Reverend Bill, is today sitting in Heaven and looking down on us—his flock, his children. And he is praying for us, yes, he is. Bill is PRAYING . . . FOR . . . US. Brother Bill is praying for us to SEE . . . THE . . . LIGHT. YES, he IS! He wants us to see the light of God's mercy, to see the light of FOR . . . GIVE . . . NESS.

"And you know what, Brother Bill is not the only person God has taken up to Heaven. Here with us today is Captain Ramrod Steel. Many of you know his wife and son, Ireme and Doray. Well Captain Steel is here to give witness today that Ireme and Doray were taken up to Heaven in The Rapture. They were taken up to Heaven, without having to suffer the pains of death, and they are there today, in Heaven, with Reverend Bill, just lookin' down on us here on earth.

"After the service today, you can come up to the front here and talk with Captain Steel. Let him tell you in his own words how his wife and son were taken by God. I think each of you should take this chance, this opportunity, to share your love with Captain Steel. Like us, he has suffered a loss, a great loss. Captain Steel's wife and son were taken up to Heaven, and he was left behind. Left here to tell us about the miracle of God's love.

"But first I want to witness to you myself. I was present at the sanctification of our friend and pastor, Reverend Doctor Bill Eous.

"I was sitting in my office Tuesday afternoon when Rev. Bill came in to speak to me. You know Bill confided in me often. He came to me with his problems; he shared with me the concerns he had for the spiritual welfare of his flock. Reverend Bill and I worked together for the spiritual growth of this community—this community of Christ.

"Bill walked into my office, and it's just like I can see him now. He stood there, with his white hair and his furrowed brow, and he smiled at me . . . he just smiled. It was like he knew what was about to happen.

"Bill said, 'God loves you Bobby. God loves you and I love you. God wants to take me, and he's going to leave you here. I know it don't seem fair, but God is callin' me Home. And while I'm gone, God wants you, Bobby, to watch over this congregation, the same way I watched over it."

"And as I sat there, a white light came out of the sky, right through the roof, and it wrapped itself around Reverend Bill. And it was just like he faded away in that big, beautiful light. His body just slowly disappeared, until there was nothing left. And the last thing I saw was his big, ol' smile, and then it faded away, too."

"But before he left us, Reverend Bill made us a video message. He didn't want us to worry about him. He just wanted us to feel God's love.

"So without any further delay, I am going to play Reverend Bill's message to his church. I pray that God gives you the wisdom and understanding to accept his message."

Rev. Bobby cued the organist, who played a hymn softly on the electric organ. Then he flipped a switch, which caused the lights to come up on the DVD player and the big screen TV. At first there was only static, then a black background faded into a picture of Rev. Bill sitting behind his desk and talking into a microphone.

"Brothers and sisters," Rev. Bill intoned, using his deep bass voice, which carried all through the chapel, "Today I want to speak to you about The Rapture."

The congregation, entranced by the face on the screen, shifted in their seats, then focused blankly as Rev. Bill continued:

"In the very near future the earth, as we know it, will change. God will come, in Power and Glory, and he will take from this earth his Chosen People. Some of you listening today will be taken away to Heaven. You will not know bodily death, as Jesus promised, but instead you will be carried physically to Heaven to be joined in perfect love with your Creator. The elderly and infirm will have their health restored. Your bodies will be transformed into the image of youth and strength. All this will happen, and soon.

"Jesus told us to watch for the signs of His coming. There will be wars and rumors of wars. We can expect terrible catastrophes to afflict us. There will be earthquakes, tidal waves, floods, famines, and terrible diseases. All these things will happen.

"But with God's love and the certainty of His Justice and His Forgiveness, we will survive. Those of us who are God's Chosen will be taken up to Heaven. But some of us, with our sins still hanging heavy on our souls, will have to stay behind.

"If the worst happens and for some reason God does not take you to Heaven to become one of His perfect creations, then you will have to live through a period of time called The Tribulation.

"During the Tribulation, God's people will be severely tested. The Antichrist will come to earth and he will rule the earth for seven ages. During this time you will face many trials and troubles. But do not despair.

"There is still a chance for you. If you are one of those who is left behind, you still have one more chance to reach Heaven and attain the perfect love waiting for you in the bosom of God. Our Lord is preparing a place for you in Heaven, a place for all those who were left behind. You simply have to place your full love and trust in Jesus. That's all you have to do. Accept Him as your personal savior. That's all it takes.

"When Jesus returns to earth and vanquishes The Antichrist, He will establish the Reign of Peace on Earth. All of mankind will know perfect love through the Purity of His Essence. Christ will establish His Kingdom, and there will be a thousand years of peace and justice on earth.

"Yes, my friends, Jesus will return to earth, trailing clouds of glory, and His Kingdom will be established, for ever and ever. Amen, and Amen."

Rev. Bill reached over to the corner of his desk, somewhere off-screen. Then the image disappeared. A mass of static filled the big screen television.

In those empty seconds, Rev. Bobby Black stood silently at his microphone. He moved his hand to wipe away a single tear, then gestured to a church elder who shut off the television.

Filled with emotion, Reerend. Bobby moved center stage, near to the now blank screen, and cued the organist to play the hymn "Come Home." The choir picked up the cue, and as Reverend Bobby spoke, they slowly whispered the lyrics, quietly, then more clearly:

"Come home, come home, you who are weary come home. Throw aside those sad regrets. You who are weary, come home."

Bobby moved forward, to the very edge of the stage, and began his closing:

"I hope Reverend Bill's message touches you the way it touched me. I feel he spoke to my heart and gave me a message of hope. Yes, the time has come. The Rapture is upon us. God has picked those of us who are perfect in his love and has taken them away to Heaven to be with him forever in paradise.

"Reverend Bill is gone, but I'm sure in these troubled days ahead he will continue to watch over us and pray on . . . I mean, for us. Reverend Bill is in Heaven. Mrs. Ireme Steel is in Heaven, too."

Bobby nodded to Ramrod, "And little Doray Steel is gone to Heaven, along with his mom. And I've heard, too, from several of you that our church secretary Mrs. Doris Morris is missing. And some of you are sure, as I am from the loving kindness of her beautiful soul, that Doris has also gone to Heaven, along with the others."

Reverend Bobby put on his glasses and took the opportunity to glance out over the congregation and measure how this news was received by the crowd. Luckily, no one seemed particularly troubled by the idea that Doris Morris was now, officially, MIA. Luckily, her husband Boris Morris hadn't come to church today.

"I hope you take Reverend Bill's message to your heart. I hope you start thinking of ways you can more fully commit your life to Jesus. We here at Mt. Saint Mary Church will be there for you. You only have to call on us.

"There won't be an offering today. There will be plenty of time for that later. But I do want you to know that we will be producing copies of Reverend Bill's message on The Rapture and making them available for a love offering of only $19.95. These and other inspirational messages of hope will be available on the Mount Saint Mary website and at the church office. Visa and MasterCard accepted.

"I look forward to seeing you on Sunday and again next Wednesday night for Bible study. In the mean time, God go with you and bless you in all your endeavors."

Rev. Bobby stepped down from the stage and went directly to Ramrod and shook his hand, pumping his arm like it was the handle of an oil well. Soon other members of the congregation came forward to express their condolences on the "loss" of his wife and son, while at the same time trying to suppress the bitterness of the idea, slowly dawning in their minds, that God had left *them* behind.

TWELVE

Early the next morning, Mark's flight landed in Dallanus, the capital city of Texrectumstan. By a strange coincidence, Mark noted a private jet landing, too. The jet was owned by the famous American industrialist Todd "Microsoft" Fox-Halburton. Interestingly enough,

Todd Fox-Halburton did not get the nickname "Microsoft" because of any connection with the Microsoft Corporation—he didn't even own any Microsoft stock. No, Todd Fox-Halburton got the nickname "Microsoft" from an ex-girlfriend, for some reason that remains a mystery.

As Mark entered the terminal, he saw a fidgety little man standing in the passageway, holding a sign that said, "Mr. Doody." Mark went up to him, and the man shifted to the left and then shifted to the right. He said, "Mr. Mark, I am your driver. I am to take you to see my master, Nickelay Dubyah. He wants to see you tonight."

The strange little man led Mark to a waiting limo, and soon both men were whisked away to the biggest hotel in the Lame Star Convention Center complex. This was where the Half Moon Party was holding its national political convention. And it was where Nickelay Dubyah the Younger was about to be nominated as his party's candidate for the office of "Fearless Leader."

* * *

Reverend Bobby Black was stunned. Word of his Wednesday night sermon had certainly gotten around.

At the Sunday morning service at least twenty "old-timers" —people who had been members of the church since the beginning—didn't show up. But in their place were at least two thousand people he had never seen before. There was barely room to seat half that many extra people. The church staff had to quickly rig up an intercom system so that Reverend Bobby's sermon could be broadcast to the crowd standing outside in the parking lot. And most important, the collection plate was up, by over 600%.

Sales of Rev. Dr. Bill Eous's "Message on The Rapture" were enormous. The website was having trouble handling all the transactions and there was a backlog on orders. People were willing to shell out a love offering of $19.95 for only the promise that a video would be mailed to them in 90 days or less. In three days, the church had taken in $36,100 in sales.

News of Reverend Bill being taken up in The Rapture spread all over Chicago. And by Sunday afternoon Reverend Bobby got a call. The Chief Elder wanted to talk to him—personally. As Bobby put the phone down, he knew that this could, and probably would, end very badly. Getting called to the Chief Elder's office was like being sent to the Principal. Only much worse.

Rev. Bobby got into his Lincoln Continental and drove across town to the Cathedral. He was met at the door by Brother Jesse and Brother Frank. They worked directly for the Chief Elder, who was on his way back from the golf course. Brothers Jesse and Frank escorted Reverend Bobby into the inner Sanctum Sanctorum of the Cathedral.

"Care for a glass of wine?" Brother Frank said.

"No, no thanks," Bobby replied.

"You might want to think about it. The Elder buys only the very best for his private stock. This bottle of wine is from a beautiful little private vineyard in The Holy Land. The Elder uses the cheap stuff only for Communion."

"No, that's okay."

"Your loss."

Bobby sank into a soft leather chair while Frank and Jesse discussed whether Steve Bartman was demon possessed, or actually a demon, while they waited for the Elder to arrive.

In Chicago, the Chief Elder of the Divine Observance of God's Grace Evangelical Church, was Elder Allyson Smith, or "Big Al" for short. Big Al had climbed the ladder to become top dog in the DOGG Evangelical Church in Illinois. But he had higher ambitions: he had his eye on becoming Supreme Elder—The Elder of Elders, Greatest of the Most High—over all the Midwest, and perhaps someday even taking over the Presidency of the Church and moving to the main offices and Holy Cathedral in New Jersey. In his heart of hearts, Big Al knew that how he handled this crisis with the Mt. Saint Mary Church could determine his future. And that's why he'd called Bobby to his office.

Reverend Bobby's hands were starting to sweat. Brother Frank and Brother Jesse were playing it cool. But Reverend Bobby could play it cool, too. He wasn't going to let himself get pushed around by these second-rate thugs. He had dealt with their kind before.

Elder Allyson swept into the room. He was a short man, stout and with a wide pleasant face that hid a steel-trap mind. Big Al waved to Bobby as he entered the room, but he deliberately avoided offering to shake his hand.

"So, you're Reverend Bobby Black," Big Al said, smiling.

"That's right, your Elderlyness . . . I mean your Eminence."

"Let's set aside the formalities for now. Is that okay with you, Bobby?"

"Sure."

"So why don't you just call me Al, okay?"

"Sure . . . Al."

"The reason I called you up here, today, is that I've heard about some interesting things going on at Mt. Saint Mary Church."

"That's right, since Reverend Bill disappeared . . ."

"Yes, Reverend Bill. I've had a few phone calls about him. And it seems a church secretary is also missing."

"That's right. They were taken up in The Rapture."

"Yes, of course. The Rapture."

The two men faced each other, Bobby in his plush leather chair and Big Al leaning against his oversized black walnut desk.

"Bobby, I have to give you credit. You've come up with a rather, shall we say 'unique' way of dealing with this problem. The question in my mind is this: Can you really pull it off?"

"Well, at church this morning we had two thousand new people show up for the service. And the collection was up 600%."

"That's certainly a sign of God's favor."

"Thank you, Al."

"But you have to realize that I have a bigger problem. As Chief Elder, I have to look at The Big Picture." He paused for emphasis. "I'm not particularly upset that you decided to go ahead . . . all on your own . . . and announce that The Rapture happened last week. It is, of course, only the most significant and anticipated event in the history of the Christian Church. It would have been nice if you could have taken the time to pick up the phone and given me a 'heads up' on this. After all, I am your Chief Elder."

"Yeah, I guess I should—"

Big Al interrupted, "Let's not dwell on the past. My main concern is for what happens *next*. You see, I have an obligation to our Church and to all the members of our denomination. Tell me, Bobby, do you ever watch *Star Trek*?"

Bobby looked at him quizically.

"Sometimes."

"In *Star Trek* they have something called 'The Prime Directive.' This is a rule that all space travelers have to abide by in dealing with primitive aliens."

"Yeah, I remember that."

"Well, they take The Prime Directive very seriously, so seriously that they would rather die than violate that Directive."

"Yeah, okay."

"In fact, if the Captain of a space vessel, even someone like Captain Kirk, if he were to violate the Prime Directive, well, that would be very, very bad."

"Okay."

"The reason I'm telling you this is that we have a Prime Directive here at DOGGE Church, too. And it's a rule that we take very, very seriously. It's very important that we, as leaders of the church, keep this rule in mind at all times."

"Okay, I didn't know we had a special rule."

"Don't worry about it, Bobby. Only the church executives are aware of the rule. You were not told because you didn't need to know. Only the top level managers and executives know about The Silver Rule."

"Silver? So it's kind of like The Golden Rule."

"Not exactly, but it's even more important than The Golden Rule. I first learned of this rule when I moved up to this Cathedral to work for Elder Doug. On my first day he took me aside and said, "Al, you have to remember one thing. It's the guiding principle of all our decisions here at the Cathedral. You must under all circumstances do everything possible to preserve the innocence of our church members. They must be able to preserve the purity of their beliefs. Their innocent faith is all they have, and we must protect it at all costs."

Bobby shifted in his leather chair.

Big Al continued, "So I am asking myself today. What can I do to preserve the innocence of our church members?"

Bobby shifted some more.

"You see my problem, Bobby? You've said some things that could seriously damage the innocent faith of our people, the little people who depend on us to protect them. I'm not saying that what you did was wrong. But you must see that I have to take steps. I have to make sure that our followers are protected in the Innocence and Purity of their belief. Let me make this clear. Unless we can come to some agreement here today, you may have to 'disappear' in The Rapture, too!"

Bobby looked over, and Frank and Jesse were smiling ear to ear.

THIRTEEN

At the entrance of the hotel, Mark could see the towering steel sculpture as it hung overhead, two gracefully designed golf clubs—each about fifty feet long and crossed so that they formed a beautiful arch. The emblem of the Crossed Golf Clubs had become the symbol of authority in the time of Nickelay the Elder. Even though he was only a mediocre player, the elder Nickelay loved golf and played golf at every opportunity. In fact, at the moment Mark passed under the archway, Nickelay the Elder was probably slicing and dicing his way across a golf course in some remote corner of Texrectumstan.

But Mark was not here to see the elder statesman. Rather, Mark was here to interview Nickelay Dubyah theYounger.

Mark made his way through the hotel, passing dozens of security men and several hundred soldiers—all of whom owed their allegiance to Dubyah's father, Nickelay the Elder. A dozen soldiers escorted Mark to the top floor of the convention center.

Dubyah the Younger was sitting in a hotel suite high above the convention room floor. He was wearing a khaki-style military uniform and a leather flight jacket—an outfit made famous by his father in his various military campaigns. Dubyah even wore the pistol that his father had made famous in his Iraqi campaign. But wearing the gun was especially important tonight. It was traditional in Texrectumstan to fire a gun in the air when accepting your party's nomination for Fearless Leader.

As he approached Dubyah, Mark remembered Dick the Welshman's warning:

"Dubyah speaks English, although it is not the language of his native land. He'll to try to converse with you. He attended an American university, so he thinks he speaks English well. Don't ask him to repeat himself, just pretend you understand what he says. He'll flounder his way through the conversation, and you're better off ignoring his odd expressions."

Beyond the seated figure, Mark noted that one long wall was solid glass, so you could stand at the wall and watch every moment of the Nominating Convention. Standing near the window was the English financier, Jonathan Seagull, and the American industrialist, Todd Fox-Haliburton. Mark noted the presence of these two men and thought to himself, "Hey, maybe they have some connection to Dubyah the Younger."

As this idea slowly rolled over in his mind, Mark looked across the room and saw Dubyah the Younger sitting in a blue upholstered chair, and next to him his American wife, a striking blonde named Lori Dubyah-Wannamaker. Lori was not wearing her usual veil, but instead had actually put on makeup and extra long eyelashes. Of course, in public she would never wear this stuff, since it was a violation of Islamic Law.

Dubyah and his friends were celebrating. Phone calls congratulating Dubyah and the Half Moon Party were coming in from all over the world. These calls were usually drowned out by the convention loudspeakers.

Dubyah sat in his chair, grinning from ear to ear as the candidates from the various provinces called out the votes for him. The Party Chairman had already figured out that the vote from the province of Waller would put Dubyah over the top and give him the party nomination. You could hear the screeching from the loudspeaker:

"From the fine old province of Hemphil, 12 votes for Ali ben Dover and 25 votes for the next Fearless Leader of Texrectumstan, Nickelay Dubyah! From the province of Ochiltree, first in the production of sheep and camels, 8 votes for Ali ben Dover and 27 votes for that great leader of men, Nickelay Dubyah! From the province of Hardin, where we have more oil wells than women, 3 votes for Ali ben Dover and 33 votes for Nickelay Dubyah!"

And finally:

"From the great big province of Waller where we have more camels than anyone and we don't need women, NO votes for Ali ben Dover and all 35 votes go to Nickelay Dubyah!!!"

The convention practically exploded with cheers as balloons fell from the ceiling.

Mark watched as Dubyah's smile grew even broader.

Then Mark glanced at Dubyah's lap. Dubyah seemed to be sporting a chubby.

Mark looked away quickly, praying that he hadn't seen what he thought he had seen, or at least that no one else in the room had noticed that Mark had looked at it.

Meanwhile, no one was more delighted with the outcome of the vote than the other candidate, Ali ben Dover. He had been having recurring nightmares about finding himself in a pit full of hungry tigers, with an angry Dubyah standing over him, wielding a titanium golf club.

* * *

Elder Allyson stood leaning against the desk in his office. Brothers Frank and Jesse were starting to fidget.

And Reverend Bobby Black was really starting to sweat.

Elder Allyson had just explained how Bobby, too, could become part of The Rapture. It was a tough spot. Unless he cooperated, Bobby was going to be raptured to the bottom of Lake Michigan, along with some iron chains and a couple of concrete blocks. With this vision before his eyes, Bobby asked:

"Well Al, what do you have in mind?"

"I've given this some thought, Bobby, and I think I've come up with a plan that will work to our mutual advantage."

Bobby breathed a sigh of relief.

"Okay."

"First, I'm going to announce tomorrow that Mt. Saint Mary Church is no longer a part of the DOGGE Church and that Mt. Saint Mary is an independent evangelical operation. The reason I'm doing this is twofold. First, if you mess up, I will need some 'plausible deniability,' as they say in the White House."

"Okay, that's fine by me."

"Second, your church is going to tithe 10% of its income to Elder Allyson's Charities, Inc., on a quarterly basis."

"Okay, that may be a tough sell to the Church Elders, but I'm pretty sure I can get them to go along."

"Good, and keep in mind that if Mt. Saint Mary Church falls behind in its payments, you're going to get a very unpleasant visit from Brother Frank and Brother Jesse."

"Okay, I get the idea. Ten percent quarterly. It's a deal."

"Good, good. Now do you have any questions? Is there anything I can help you with?"

"Well Al, I hate to bring this up. But I do have a problem that maybe you can do something about."

"Sure. What is it?"

"When Reverend Eous was Raptured, about $375,000 vanished along with him."

"I see. That is a problem."

"I'm expecting an audit from the main office in New Jersey. The examiner is coming here in two weeks."

"Since Mt. Saint Mary is now no longer a part of this denomination, the visit from the Examiner's Office can be cancelled. I'll see to it myself."

"Good. But what happens when the bookkeeper at Mt. Saint Mary looks at the books? I won't be able to hide the missing money for very long."

"Really, Bobby, you are a novice in these things. I'll send my own auditor, Mr. Arthur, over to the church tomorrow to straighten out your books."

"But how is he going to hide the missing money?"

"That's nothing. During his career in the oil and gas industry, Mr. Arthur hid billions of dollars in offshore accounts. He's a genius at this kind of stuff."

"But if he can't . . . Is there any way you could loan us the money?"

"Bobby, Bobby, Bobby, we're tapped out at the moment. We've had to settle a lot of lawsuits recently.

"You remember Reverend Anderson, from over at Mission Hills Church? We had a real struggle keeping the stories about him and those Boy Scouts out of the newspapers. And the money we had to pay out to the families, not to mention what we had to pay out to the lawyers. . . .

"We just don't have that kind of cash lying around right now."

"So, what can we do? How can we hide the missing cash?"

"I suppose Mr. Arthur can make it look like Mt. Saint Mary paid the denomination $375,000 for the church building and property it sits on."

"Hey, that might just work."

"Just leave all of this in Mr. Arthur's hands. He's really quite good. Just keep in mind that you'll want to tip him an additional 50% of his fee, under the table."

"Okay, thanks Al. You've been a big help."

"And of course, Bobby, there will be times in the future when I may need to call on you for a favor."

"A favor. What kind of favor?"

"For example, I have a minister here on staff who is just coming out of alcohol rehab. He has a serious problem."

Sensing trouble, Bobby squirmed. "What kind of problem?"

"Well, he has a fondness for 20-year-old Scotch whiskey and 16-year-old Asian girls."

Bobby's face fell as he realized that he was now going to have to deal with a minister who had a history of chasing booze and babes.

Big Al continued, "We're all hoping that he can learn to split the difference and find happiness with 18-year-olds."

FOURTEEN

Ramrod Steel slowly woke from a bad dream. Sunday morning had come and gone, and he had missed his chance to attend morning services at his wife's church, on his own, without being blackmailed with the promise of food or sex. It was a strange feeling for Ramrod, lying on the bed without the anticipation of sexual activity, or even the possibility of guilt-free sex. The idea of calling Hadshe flickered in his mind, for a moment, before being washed away by the overwhelming need to urinate.

Coming out of the bathroom, he heard the noise of Cloye in the kitchen, slamming pots and pans together as she tried to make French toast, or something. Suddenly Ramrod realized that he was hungry, so he slipped on his housecoat and trundled down the stairs, searching for food.

Earlier that morning Cloye had made toast and scrambled eggs, which were now sitting on the counter—three hours old—and floating in a plate full of grease. Now Cloye was working on a pan of macaroni & cheese, while also searching for her mother's cookbook.

Ramrod had given his wife a *Precocious Minutes Cookbook* a year ago at Christmas, but for some reason Ireme still preferred the old *Betty Crocker Cookbook* she had owned for years, the one he had given her shortly after they were married.

Walking into the kitchen, Ramrod sniffed around the cold eggs. An idea popped into his head, “Hey, maybe I should invite Hadshe out for supper.”

At the moment he thought the words, they also came out of his mouth.

Cloye glared at her father.

“Hadshe who?”

“Uh . . . Hadshe. She’s a flight attendant I know. I’ve been thinking about inviting her to our church.”

“You mean Mom’s church.”

“I mean our church. We are all members . . . or you could be if you agreed to get baptized.”

“Not gonna happen.”

“I mean, it’s not that big a deal. You put on the baptismal gown and walk down into the water tank. It’s in the alcove right next to where the choir stands. And then the minister puts his hand on the small of your back and lowers you under the water. It’s easy.”

“If it’s so easy, why haven’t you done it yet?”

“Well, I’m still working up to it. It just takes me a while to get organized. I’ve been pretty busy, you know, lately.”

“I tell you what, Dad. You get baptized and I’ll think about it.”

“Well okay, I guess that’s fair.”

Ramrod shoved the greasy eggs into his mouth and immediately began wondering about where his next meal was coming from. He hoped that Cloye could, at least, leave him some macaroni and cheese for later. But even more important, Ramrod slowly realized that now, with Ireme in Heaven, he was both legally and morally a free man. He could pursue Hadshe or anyone else he wanted to. Having a wife taken away to Heaven was like being both “single” and “married”—but without all the annoying restrictions.

* * *

As Jesse and Frank escorted Rev. Bobby from the office of His Eminence, Big Al had an idea. He called the main church office in New Jersey and asked to speak directly to The President.

It was Sunday afternoon, so his secretary had to page The President at the golf course, but in less than half an hour, President Timothy Nixon was on the horn with Big Al.

"Tim, I think I've got the solution to that 'little problem' we were talking about last week."

The President coughed into the receiver. "You mean the pedophile ministers?"

"Yeah, that's right. I've just figured out a way to make that problem disappear!"

* * *

Ramrod slowly put on his gray suit and added the gold cufflinks that Ireme had given him for their first anniversary. She'd bought him the cufflinks back in the days when he was still a US Air Force pilot. Money was pretty scarce back then, but Ramrod had been happy to live on love. And what about Ireme?

In Ramrod's view, Ireme lived for her husband. Shortly after she joined her new church, Ireme went to a church seminar on The Vocation of Women. She came home that day and told Ramrod that she wished she could do more than just wash his clothes, make his meals, raise his kids and clean his home—she wished she could breathe for him, too. It was like she couldn't do enough for her family, that they just weren't happy enough. People could always be more happy than they were. And that's why they needed more of Jesus in their lives.

The idea of Ireme and her single-minded devotion—it all floated about in Ramrod's mind as he slipped on his gray overcoat and walked out to the car. Cloye was not going with him to the Sunday night church service. But that was okay. Ramrod had called Hadshe and arranged to meet her for supper later that night.

As Ramrod drove to church, he thought about Ireme and about Hadshe. He said out loud, "I think the church should have some sort of memorial service for Irem." And then he added, "I sure would hate to go to the service by myself."

GIVEN THE CIRCUMSTANCES, Big Al had no trouble convincing the President of the Church to go along with his idea. Big Al could hear it in his voice, Tim Nixon was desperate.

The DOGG Evangelical Church had been the victim of dozens of frivolous lawsuits from families alleging that their children had been molested by ministers. The situation had gotten so bad that the Church, itself, appeared to be on the verge of bankruptcy.

President Nixon had his own lobbyists working with the lobbyists for the Catholic bishops. They wanted to get laws passed in various state legislatures that would limit the number of lawsuits and the award amounts. Several states had already passed laws making it impossible to file a lawsuit unless "the plaintiff has undergone severe psychological damage that makes in impossible for him or her to hold a job." Other states were quickly, thanks to intense ecumenical lobbying, passing laws that limited the dollar amount of awards that could be sought in these cases. Still other states were imposing strict time limits on how long a victim could wait before filing a lawsuit.

But all these efforts were coming too late to help the DOGG Evangelical Church. The national headquarters in New Jersey was in hock, with a second and third mortgage on the cathedral.

Under the circumstances, President Nixon was more than happy to give Big Al everything he wanted. And Big Al wanted Reggie Agnew's job.

Tim Nixon forced Supreme Elder Reggie Agnew into early retirement, beginning next summer, which would soon make Elder Allyson Smith the second most powerful man in the DOGG Evangelical Church. Big Al was going to be Supreme Elder over the entire Midwest, from Ohio to Colorado. If his plan succeeded, Big Al was to be named Elder of Elders, Greatest of the Most High.

Big Al took charge immediately. He made a TO DO list.

1. Contact headquarters and get a list of terminally ill, retired ministers. Find out which are near death and fly them to Pueblo, Colorado for a "Health Care Summit."

2 Contact the DOGG Evangelical Church retirement village in Colorado, today, and tell them to order ten year's worth of stationery. Also, let them know they are hosting a summit.

3. Contact the main office in New Jersey, tomorrow, and tell them to officially change the name of the retirement village in Colorado to "Heaven Retirement Home."

4. Get a list of all the "problem" ministers who have not yet had lawsuits filed against them. Arrange for all of them to fly to Pueblo, Colorado—arriving there no later than Tuesday night.

5. Arrange for a bus to meet the ministers in Pueblo on Wednesday morning. Arrange for a second bus to be in Dodge City, Kansas.

6. Call Rev. Bobby Black—Now!

Big Al looked on his list, and he found that it was good.

* * *

Mark waited quietly as Nickelay Dubyah's supporters cheered and drank toasts of (supposedly) non-alcoholic beer to the new nominee of the Half Moon Party. Mark hesitated about taking a beer. Seeing his hesitation, one of Dubyah's men whispered in Mark's ear, "This is fermented swill. They will serve the good stuff at a private party later on."

Mark was glad to be invited to the private party for Dubyah, but he really wanted to get on with his interview. He thought, "They should treat me with more respect. This is a helluvah way to treat the winner of the Ernest Hemingway Prize for War Correspondence!" As Dubyah's generals crowded around him, Mark fumed "I've probably seen more military action than half these yokels! These jerks probably never even heard of Ernest Hemingway."

Meanwhile Dubyah posed for pictures, holding aloft the famous titanium golf club that his father had given him. Mark had seen photos of dozens of places in Texrectumstan where there were full-sized portraits of Dubyah and his golf club, enormous billboards with Dubyah and the golf club, and even a dozen or so statues of Nickelay Dubyah and his golf club.

Several years ago Dubyah's press secretary put out the story during the second Iraq War that Dubyah had single-handedly beaten to death a battalion of Sodom Hussein's crack infantry with this golf club. The story of Dubyah attacking a group of heavily armed Iraqi soldiers with only a golf club sounded a lot like the story of Samson slaying the Philistines, and like that famous story it did include someone getting jawboned by an ass.

But, in reality, during the Iraq War, Dubyah had spent the entire time drinking and carousing with the Texrectumstan National Guard.

Generally, Dubyah was known for avoiding personal danger, having the same self-preservation instinct that guides the huge cockroaches native to Texrectumstan

Eventually Dubyah tired of the endless high fives and the back-slapping. He invited Mark into a small private room in his suite.

"Well, Mr. Mark, we are finally alone."

Dubyah's speech was slurred, and Mark suspected that he had already been celebrating—a lot.

"So, Mr. Mark, what questions can I answer for you?"

"Well, your Majesty, are you at all surprised by the way you handily won the nomination of the Half Moon Party?"

"No, no. It was shooting ducks in a barrel."

"I think most of my readers would agree with you. And do you expect to win the national election just as easily?"

"Sure. Why not."

"Well, in my country politicians are usually a bit more shy about predicting success."

"Here in my country we always know ahead of time how the election will come out. If we don't know, then we don't have the election."

"Oh, so your elections are more like the elections in Britain."

"Yes. We make sure no one win who shouldn't win. It would weaken the political parties to have elections and no one know who going to win."

"I see. And what plans do you have for the future. What will you do once you are elected Fearless Leader?"

"I have world for the . . . plans, plans for the world. Start with old Soviet Union."

At that moment a bodyguard entered the room and escorted Dubyah out to see his waiting supporters. Mark could hear the shouts of "New World Order! New World Order! New World Order!" as they echoed back through the halls.

FIFTEEN

Reverend Bobby Black answered the phone and heard the one voice he really, really didn't want to hear.

Big Al had a "little job" for him. For some reason Big Al wanted Bobby to proclaim in his Sunday night sermon that The Rapture was still going on. Bobby thought this was a little dangerous, and it certainly wasn't very Biblical, but—what the hey—Bobby owed Big Al a favor.

That night there was a somewhat larger crowd at the church than at the morning service. The technicians rigged up extra speakers and cameras and microphones. There were extra televisions set up in the three chapels. All three were in use, and yet it was still Standing Room Only.

Reverend Bobby made sure to greet Captain Steel at the front door. He was disappointed that Ramrod had missed the morning service, but it was more important that Captain Steel be seen here now. This was going to be an even harder sell than a few days ago. Today Bobby had to take his church into new, uncharted territory. He had to convince them that The Rapture was an ongoing event and that people could still, even now, be carried away to Heaven.

As the congregation moved into their pews or their folding chairs, there was a sense of expectation in the air. Reverend Bobby walked down the aisle and shook hands with several of the old timers. To most people the television camera would be a distraction, but to Bobby Black the camera was his best and most faithful friend.

Bobby started off the service with the hymns "The Old, Rugged Cross" and "We Shall Gather at the River." As soon as the congregation heard the opening chords of the first hymn they knew that Bobby meant business. This was serious stuff!

After the second hymn, Bobby launched into his message: "Brothers and Sisters, here I stand before you. I'm so excited. And I just can't hide it! There is a new world beginning here for us tonight. There is a vast new world to conquer, for Jesus!

"This afternoon I went to see Elder Allyson at the Cathedral and witnessed to him about Reverend Bill Eous and The Rapture. Elder Allyson and I sat down together, and we prayed together over this. Yes, we prayed and prayed, asking God to show us His Truth."

Bobby dropped to his knees.

"That's right. I got DOWN on my knees next to Elder Allyson and we prayed and prayed for an answer. And you know what? God gave us His answer. God gave us His message for this church.

"And this is the amazing thing. This is the New World I mentioned before. God spoke to me. God gave me a message. It's a message that He wants us to share WITH THE WHOLE WORLD.

"God told me that The Rapture is STILL GOING ON TODAY. Most educated people think that The Rapture is just a one-time event. They think that—WHAM! BAM! And the whole thing is over and done with.

"But that's not true. No, The Rapture is not over. And it doesn't matter what any of the scholars tell you. The Rapture is NOT over. It's not over until God says it's over.

"When Daniel was cast into the lion's den, was it over? NO! It wasn't over.

"When Pharaoh sent Moses into the Wilderness, was it over? NO! It wasn't over.

"And when Jesus was nailed up on the cross, was it over? NO! It wasn't over.

"It's not over until God's people say it's over! HALLELUJAH! And Amen."

There was a chorus of Amens from the congregation. The crowd was visibly stirred by the sincerity and emotion in his voice. Reverend Bobby cued the choir, and they began singing in a muted voice, "How Long Must We Wait?"

Long have we sought e-ter-nal life.
Years have we wait-ed in sin and strife;
In darkness groped, sad mis-ry's mate,
How long? how long must we wait?

Bobby lowered his arm and the choir dropped to a light hum.

"Friends, The Rapture is still going on today. God's people are still being taken up to Heaven. The Rapture may take several days. It may take weeks. It might even take years. NO ONE KNOWS how LONG The Rapture will last.

"And so you ask me, Brother Bobby, what about me? When will Jesus come for me? When will Jesus COME . . . FOR . . . ME?"

Bobby put his hand to his heart, and a pained expression crossed his face.

"And I'll say, 'Look to the Bible. It tells you right there.' Look at John chapter 21, verse 20 through 24."

Reverend Bobby grabbed his black leather Bible from the podium and swept down to the front of the stage, waving the book and pointing to the sky, in his best imitation of the great evangelist, Billy Graham. By now the hot lights were making him sweat, and he could feel his white cotton shirt where it was sticking against his chest and his armpits.

"In the Gospel of John, we have the story of Christ talking to Peter. He tells Peter that one day Peter will die. Then Peter asks, 'What about that guy? What will happen to your Beloved Disciple?' And then Christ says, 'What's it to you? If I want him to wait here until I return, then he will wait around here until I come back.'

"In this way Christ is telling Peter, and He is telling all of us, that HE will decide what will happen to us, and He will decide in His own good time. If Jesus wants us to die and be buried in the ground while our souls are carried to Heaven, then that's what's gonna happen. But, if Jesus wants us to stand around and wait until He comes back, then we'll stand around and wait until he comes back.

"And if Jesus wants to take us up in The Rapture, all at one time, He'll do it that way. And if he wants to take us up a few at a time, picking and choosing the best—just like my mother does when she's buying cantaloupe at the market—then Jesus can do that, too!"

There were laughs from the audience, followed by Amens.

"Jesus said in the Gospel of John that if He wants it that way, His disciples will wait for Him UNTIL HE COMES. And it's the same for all of us. We must wait UNTIL HE COMES. We must, like the Beloved Disciple, be content to wait until He comes FOR US.

"Yes, Brothers and Sisters, Hallelujah and praise God. The miracle of The Rapture is happening right now, as I speak to you. Across the world thousands of Christians are being taken up into Heaven.

God's angels are carrying them away. Every day the True Believers in Jesus, our Lord and Savior, are being carried UP TO GOD!

"And you, all of you sitting hear today. You still have a chance to be carried up to Heaven, just like Brother Bill, just like Sister Ireme. Even the little children will be called unto Him, just like little Doray Steel. Yes, even now you have a chance to escape the Torments of Hellfire. You have a chance to find peace in Abraham's bosom."

Rev. Bobby stepped down from the platform and went directly to Ramrod Steel. Bobby smiled and put his hand on Ramrod's shoulder.

"You still have a chance to find eternal happiness with your loved ones. Won't you take this opportunity to make your peace with God?"

Bobby stepped back, then cued the organist who quietly began to play "I Will Rise and Go to Jesus" while the choir sang, faintly:

Come, ye sin-ners, poor and need-y,
Weak and wound-ed, sick and sore;
Je-sus read-y stands to save you,
Full of pit-y, love and pow'r.

and then more faintly:

I will a-rise and go to Je-sus
He will em-brace me in His arms;
In the arms of my dear Sav-ior,
Oh, there are ten thousand charms.

"Friends, brothers and sisters, you need to find Peace with The Lord. I'll be waiting here for you, right here. Come on up. Dedicate your life to Christ. It's time to come Home. Don't you know where your home is? It's time, now. It's time to come home."

Ramrod Steel staggered to his feet, blubbering like a baby. He walked up the aisle to Bobby and put his arms around him and hugged him—but in a manly way. Bobby turned Ramrod around and had him stand near him. By then, dozens of others were coming forward, ready to dedicate their lives to Christ.

The people streamed forward as the choir started to sing softly, "Calling You Home" with its refrain of "Call-ing you home, call-ing you home, Je-sus my Savior is call-ing, call-ing you home."

The people moved forward down the aisles, like sheep moving down a chute at the stockyard. Once again, Reverend Bobby had pulled the proverbial fat out of the fire.

IREME STEEL AND DORAY spent Sunday night walking home from a small evangelical church service in an old storefront in downtown Branson. Ireme had settled into her new job at the food court, but she was worried about Doray. She couldn't send for his birth certificate, much less his school records. She couldn't do anything that might alert the authorities to the fact that she and Doray were in Branson.

On her first day at work, Ireme took a bus to The Precocious Minutes Theme Park. As an employee of one of the many attractions in Branson, Ireme got a special discount bus ticket, not to mention special discounts on tickets to the various shows. But Ireme was mainly interested in doing God's work, and that meant being a faithful employee of 7th Heaven Bar-B-Qued Angelic Wings in the food court.

Ireme couldn't believe how lucky she was to work here. The beautiful artwork at PMTP always choked her up. From the giant bronze Precocious Minutes Angel statuary in the water fountain at the front gate, to the swirling stained glass of the Precocious Minutes Chapel. It was all just too beautiful to believe. There were times, looking at the long hallway of the chapel, when all Ireme could think of was her all-time favorite movie: *The Wizard of Oz*. It was like PMTP was The Emerald City of Oz, come to life, but without the green little people.

Ireme looked forward to next Wednesday, which was Family Day. She could finally bring Doray to PMTP for free, so that he could see for himself the beauty and splendor of God's creation.

* * *

After the service, Bobby took Ramrod to his new office, the main pastor's office that had only a week ago belonged to Reverend Bill Eous. But Rev. Bill was called Home by God. And so Bobby now inherited Reverend Bill's office, his library, and his huge collection of sermons on tape and DVD. Reverend. Bill recorded many of his best sermons, and so Bobby had plenty of titles to choose from.

Bobby gave Ramrod a copy of Reverend Bill's famous "Message on the Rapture" DVD and a copy of "Rapture 2: the Message Continues." A hundred boxes of Rapture 2 had just been delivered to the church that morning by a local tape and DVD duplicating service. Rev. Bobby asked Ramrod to watch the tapes at home sometime soon. Bobby was sure that Reverend Bill's message would strengthen Ramrod's faith. He also hinted that it would be nice if Cloye would watch the tapes, too.

As Ramrod left the church, climbing into his car in the almost empty parking lot, the last light in the church blinked out. As was his habit, Bobby Black was the last person to leave the church after a Sunday night service.

Standing in the parking lot, Bobby could feel his body still vibrating from adrenaline. It was like a powerful electric charge running up and down, head to foot. As Bobby held his hands out in front of him, he could see the muscles and nerves still twitching, and the sweat was still hot where his cotton shirt and white cotton boxers clung to his body.

As Bobby reached his car, he saw a light go on inside a little white Toyota parked a few spaces away from his Lincoln. When the light came on, he could see two young women—actually two fine young women—sitting in the car. One of the women—Bobby could see now that they were nearly identical twins—stepped out of the car and waved to him.

"Reverend Bobby! Hey, Reverend Bobby. Where're you going?"

"Hi, girls. I was just going to my apartment."

Dee, one of the sisters, said, "Well, you know, you could come over to our place. We're having a party. It's a small party. And we thought you might want to come along."

"I'd love to; but, you know, I was under those hot lights and I'm still pretty sweaty from it. What if I go take a shower and then come over to your place?"

The second sister, Ann, opened her car door and stepped out. She stood, leaning provocatively against the car, and said, "No, don't do that Bobby. We want you just the way you are."

"You mean," Bobby said, "just as I am?"

It was a short distance to the girls' apartment, and Bobby rode in the back seat with Ann, while Dee drove the little stick-shift Toyota. Bobby hummed to himself the old hymn, "Just as I am":

Just as I am, Thine own to be,
Friend of the young, who lov-est meeeee

Then Ann joined in:

Just as I am, young, strong and free,
To be the best that I can be
For truth, and righteousness, and Thee,
Lord of my life, I come

Soon they were all singing together, and they made a sweet, sweet sound.

Dee and Ann lived in a brick apartment house with a security door and Spanish-style iron steps going up to the second floor. Bobby walked with Dee on one arm and Ann on the other. Ann unlocked the door while Dee pressed her bosom against Bobby's arm.

Once inside, Ann went into the kitchen and brought back three bottles of beer, "Hey, Bobby, you look like you could use a cold one."

Bobby took off the cap and thought, "and it looks like I got a couple o' hot ones as part of the deal."

Dee went over to the stereo and put on some jazz, while Ann maneuvered Bobby over to the white leather sofa. Soon Ann was sitting, practically on top of Bobby, while pulling his hair with her right hand, kissing him, and unbuttoning his shirt with her left.

Dee disappeared for a few minutes, then returned with a video camera mounted on a tripod.

Bobby stopped and said, "What's that for?"

"We like to take videos of ourselves. You don't mind, do you?"

"Hey, Babe, that sounds like fun. Do I get to shoot a video of you two together?"

"Sure, honey."

"Awesome!"

Dee joined Bobby and Ann on the enormous leather sofa.

Soon, all three had lost most of their clothes. Bobby had Ann pressed under him on the sofa when the CD player changed, abruptly, to "Onward, Christian Soldiers." Bobby managed to make good use of the martial rhythms of the old hymn. He was pounding away, his body glistening with sweat, as the stereo beat out:

Onward Christian soldiers, Marching as to war,
With the cross of Je-sus Go-ing on be-fore!
Christ, the roy-al Mas-ter, Leads a-gainst the foe;
For-ward in-to bat-tle, See, His banner go!

and then the refrain:

Onward Christian soldiers, Marching as to war
With the cross of Je-sus Go-ing on be-fore!

Bobby pretty quickly got the rhythm of it, and finished verses 2 through 4:

At the sign of tri-umph Satan's host doth flee;
On then Christian soldiers, On to victory!
Hell's foun-da-tions quiv-er At the shout of praise;
Brothers, lift your voices, Loud your anthems raise!

Like a mighty ar-my Moves the Church of God;
Brothers, we are treading Where the saints have trod
We are not di-vid-ed; All one bod-y we
One in hope and doc-trine, One in char-i-ty

And each time the rousing refrain:

Onward Christian soldiers, Marching as to war
With the cross of Je-sus Go-ing on be-fore!

At the end of the last verse, Bobby was overcome with exuberance and the fruits (actually vanilla yogurt) of his desire spewed forth.

Dee tried to adjust the camera angle to film the "money shot" but missed it. She was pretty pissed off and swore under her breath, then yelled, "Hey! Bobby, nobody said 'Come, All Ye Faithful' did they?"

* * *

Ramrod Steel left the church, carrying his copies of the videos "Rapture" and "Rapture 2: the Message Continues" Reverend Bobby had given them to him—for free! He was glad that Rev. Bobby had no hard feelings about the fact that Ramrod had neglected the church so much over the past two years. It just seemed to Ramrod that Ireme was doing enough for the church to cover both of them. The fact that she was taken up in The Rapture while Ramrod was left behind was like a not-so-subtle hint to him that God wanted him to be more involved in church work, too.

Staying behind had been his mistake, but Ramrod was happy to make up for it now. He wanted to be baptized and become a prominent member of the church. He wanted to teach Sunday School classes, too, and he planned to start reading Doray's Precocious Minutes Bible as soon as he got home.

Then it hit him. He had made a date with Hadshe! In fact, he was already a half-hour late in meeting her at the IHOP. Seconds later, Ramrod scrambled to his car and took off out of the parking lot like it was a runway at O'Hare. He was only five minutes away from the IHOP, but Ramrod was sure that Hadshe would be very annoyed with him for arriving late.

When he got to the restaurant, he pulled into a spot near the front door and rushed in. Hadshe was already seated in a booth, nestled discreetly near the Ladies' Room.

"Sorry I'm late," Ramrod said. "I was held up at church by Rev. Black. He wanted to give me a couple of videos on The Rapture."

"The what?"

"The Rapture. At the end of the world, before Christ returns, many Christians will be taken up in The Rapture."

"Really?" Hadshe suppressed a smile.

"Yeah, and Rev. Black thinks it's already started."

"What's already started?"

"The Rapture. People being taken up to Heaven. They just disappear, like my wife."

"I thought your wife left you."

"Well, she did. She was taken up to Heaven by God. Now she's in Heaven with Jesus, and Moses and the rest of those guys. And my son Doray is gone, too."

Hadshe gave him a look that said, "Hoo Boy, did I pick a nut job." But Ramrod blundered on, talking about the Last Days and the Second Coming (which at that very moment, Brother Bobby Black was experiencing).

"Anyway . . ." Ramrod said, his mind wandering. Then his gaze wandered over to the building across the street, the Womyn's Health Clinic.

"Hey," he said. "My wife used to picket there all the time."

"Really, why did she do that?"

"Why?" Ramrod's mind floundered around for a few moments. "Uh, because they do abortions over there."

"No they don't," Hadshe said.

"Well, maybe they used to."

"No, my sister works at an abortion clinic downtown. There are only a few in Chicago, and the Womyn's Health Clinic isn't one of them."

"Oh, well I'm sure they do bad stuff over there."

"Like what?"

"I don't know, but I'm sure Ireme wouldn't picket over there for no reason."

"Well, they probably counsel women on birth control."

"Yeah, that's probably it. They give out rubbers and stuff."

"But, Rammy, didn't you and your wife use birth control?"

"What? Hell no."

"But you were married twenty years and you have only two children. You must have used birth control . . . unless you have a fertility problem."

"A fertility problem. No, I don't have a problem. I can get it up anytime and all the time. In the morning I can't even bend it with one hand."

"No, I said a fertility problem, not an erectile dysfunction."

"Fertility. I don't think so. Ireme would have said something."

Hadshe stopped for a moment, then reached across the table, taking Ramrod's hand.

"Rammy, when you and Ireme were going to be . . . intimate, did she go to the bathroom first?"

"Well, yeah, I guess so. Why?"

"Do you think she might have gone to the bathroom to put in her diaphragm?"

"A diaphragm? I don't know. I always thought she was going to the bathroom to put on a little perfume."

"Well, I think you need to face the fact that your wife was using birth control. Otherwise you and she would have had ten children by now, not two."

Hadshe gave him "the look" and Ramrod realized that she pitied him—for some strange reason that he couldn't understand. As the fog of ideas floated through his mind, Hadshe finished her chocolate Sunday and stood up.

"Listen, Rammy. I have a flight early tomorrow, so I have to get going. But why don't you give me a call? Soon."

"Okay."

Hadshe left the IHOP and even paid for Ramrod's coffee. Meanwhile, Ramrod sat in his booth wondering how Ireme could have kept something this important from him for so many years.

* * *

For Mark Doody, getting to cover the convention party was the opportunity of a lifetime. It made all those years he spent in college almost worthwhile.

Five years ago, Mark had gotten a B.A. in Journalism from BJU, a private college in the Southwest. It took the better part of six years, and they were mostly a waste. Mark knew lots of information, but lacked the discernment to figure out what it all meant. In that sense, he was a perfect journalist. That is, he would repeat whatever he was told by government bureaucrats or corporate press agents without asking any embarrassing questions or adding any awkward embellishments. He believed fully and completely everything he was told. Essentially, Mark Doody was a blank slate—but with a pretty face that seemed to radiate "honesty" for the television cameras. At the same time, Mark's "Liberal" education made him a fount of useless information on all sorts of topics.

For example, Mark was one of the few people who knew that the hymn "Onward, Christian Soldiers" was written in the 19th century by a scholar named Sabine Baring-Gould. Reverend Baring-Gould was the author of over a hundred books, including histories, theology, and even folklore. In fact, his second most famous work (after "Onward, Christian Solders") was a book on werewolves. Rev. Sabine Baring-Gould firmly believed in the existence of werewolves, and he considered them to be proof of the power of Satan on earth.

Baring-Gould was a fairly typical 19th-century Christian scholar in this respect. For example, John Ruskin, the famous Victorian scholar, firmly believed in the existence of Dragons, just as he believed in the existence of Satan, and he once wrote:

"There, however, our Dragon does not fail us, both Carpaccio and Tinoret having the deepest convictions on that subject;—as all strong men must have; for the Dragon is too true a creature, to all such, spiritually. That it is indisputably a living and venomous creature, materially, has been the marvel of the world, innocent and guilty, not knowing what to think of the Terrible Worm; nor whether to worship it, as the Rod of their lawgiver, or to abhor it as the visible symbol of the everlasting Disobedience."

This and other interesting, but essentially useless, bits of data were acquired by Mark during his college days, working in the library at BJU. But none of it prepared him for the confrontation he was going to have one day with Nickelay Dubyah the Younger, future Fearless Leader of Texrectumstan—and perhaps even (to some) the physical embodiment of that Terrible Worm imagined by Ruskin.

But we get ahead of ourselves.

While Mark sat in the press room, he could see through the darkened glass wall that the Half Moon Party's national convention was getting wound up for the climax: Nickelay Dubyah the Younger was about to address his party and accept their nomination for the job of Fearless Leader. As the night wore on, each speaker became more loud and strident than the previous one. Mark could hear the cheers as the name "Nickelay Dubyah" was yelled over and over.

A young man approached Mark and handed him a press packet. Inside was the text of Nickelay's acceptance speech, translated into English, French, German, and Russian.

Suddenly there was a rousing cheer as a young woman walked on stage, leading a donkey. Mark thought this a bit odd. Wasn't the Tiger the mascot for the Half Moon Party? Or was it the Elephant?

Well, as long as no one gets hurt . . . at least they didn't execute politicians on stage, the way they did when Nickelay the Elder was in power.

Mark decided to take this opportunity to read through Dubyah's speech. This text and accompanying stage directions would be put on the teleprompter for Dubyah to read. Dubyah, of course, would stumble through the speech and follow the stage directions like a trained seal. The speech was pretty much the typical political boiler-plate speech, just like you would hear in any national campaign in the United States. But Mark's eyes almost bulged out of his head when he saw some of the stage directions.

The speech read:

"People of Texrectumstan, I, your friend and neighbor, accept the nomination of my party for the job of Fearless Leader.

(pause for cheers)

"In a few weeks the people will go to the polls and elect a new leader. I am sure of victory, as you are. Our polls show that I will win, with 97.3% of the vote.

(pause for cheers — wave right hand)

"With thanks to Heaven, and the help of my smarter brother, Jebbulah, this nation will have a new mandate to gather together the wealth of our country.

(pause for cheers — wave left hand)

"No longer will our country's wealth be squandered on propping up the poor and the unworthy. Our future lies in strength, not weakness.

(pause for cheers — smile — wave both hands)

"We will have as our foremost goal the enhancement of our racial purity. We will drive the mongrel races from our country so that our people may enjoy the purity of a True Islam.

(pause — take gun from holster)

"With Allah as our guide, the now weak and degenerate states of the former Soviet Union will join with us as our allies, and we will begin to establish a New World based on the belief that all men are created equal.

(pause — smile — raise gun next to head, muzzle pointing up)

"While at the same time, we recognize that some people are more equal than others.

(pause — continue to hold gun pointing up)

"My friends, the Half Moon Party represents the future of Texrectumstan. We will go down in history as the Founding Fathers of the New World Order.

(pause — smile — pull trigger)

"Our enemies in the Full Moon Party will go down to defeat. Heaven guides the will of the people. Please repeat after me: I pledge allegiance to the Half Moon Party of Texrectumstan and the Democracy which it Prepares. We are one nation, under Allah, with Wealth and Power, forever and forever. Amen."

Mark stared at the paper, trying to figure out what all this meant. He could hear Nickelay's voice, carried across the tinny-sounding speaker system. Then he looked at Dubyah's visage through the darkened glass. Dubyah had pulled his gun from its holster and was raising it, his finger on the trigger, when he stumbled. As Dubyah was falling to the floor behind the podium, Mark heard the gun go off, and then there was pandemonium. People were yelling, screaming, and scrambling wildly for the exits. Mark looked toward the podium and saw Nickelay Dubyah's body splayed out on the floor, with blood oozing from his head where the gunshot wound was still smoking from the powder flash.

Mark was too stunned to move. Even with his many weeks of combat experience, embedded with the sailors of the Abraham Lincoln, nothing had prepared him for this! Was Dubyah—The Antichrist—now lying there dead from a self-inflicted wound? If so, how did this fit in with Biblical prophecy?

In fact, Tragedy was avoided that night, as the shot was deflected by a steel plate in Dubyah's skull (the result of an earlier assassination attempt).

The Texrectumstanian version of the Secret Service rushed onto the stage and snatched away the pistol, before any further damage could be done. A shocked and awed Dubyah, supported by two of his bodyguards, was led off stage, with a third holding a towel to Dubyah's head wound. This was accompanied by rousing cheers from what was left of the gathered Half Moon Party members, loudly rejoicing at their candidate's narrow escape from death.

The next day the Texrectumstanian Secret Police rounded up a dozen leaders of the Full Moon Party and put them up against the wall.

The cable news channel WWN announced that Nickelay Dubyah had narrowly escaped an assassination attempt and that members of an enemy terrorist cell had been arrested and executed.

A newsletter published by a small, radical Christian sect in Wisconsin noted that Dubyah, like The Antichrist predicted in the Holy Scripture, had survived a near-fatal wound to the head.

SIXTEEN

Ramrod sat alone for several minutes at the IHOP in Mt. Saint Mary, Illinois. The waitress was a platinum blond with a too-tight lavender skirt. She leaned forward and gave him a full view of her tightly packed cleavage. She obviously knew Victoria's Secret and used it to her full advantage.

"You feelin' okay, Hon?" she said as she filled Ramrod's coffee cup until it (nearly) runneth over.

"I'll be okay. It's just that I've had a long day."

"Say, aren't you Ireme Steel's husband?"

"You know Ireme?" Ramrod said, a slight quiver in his voice.

"Yeah, sure. She comes in here all the time. She pickets the clinic across the street. Yeah, she always comes in here on Friday afternoon and orders apple pie and a glass of milk. And she showed me her photographs, too. That's how I recognized you."

"Oh."

"How is she doing? I didn't see her last Friday."

"She's gone."

"Gone. You mean she's on vacation?"

"No, I mean she's gone away. Forever."

"She left you. I can't hardly believe that. She was always tellin' me what a great husband and father you are. And she hinted about your finer qualities, too."

"Well, you might as well know. Ireme was taken up in The Rapture."

"Really? Wow, I'd like to have seen that."

"Wait? You know about The Rapture?"

"Sure, I was raised a PK, a preacher's kid. I know all about the End Times and Revelation and all that stuff."

"Do . . . do you believe in it?"

"Absolutely. That's why I'm workin' here as a waitress instead of going back to college and tryin' to get a business degree. Why should I go to school, when the End Times are comin' any day now?

"Could I talk to you? I'm still a little bit new at this stuff. I mean, you know, I grew up in a Christian family and all that, but I never really got involved in trying to convert other people. I don't think I ever did really try to. I mean except for those times in high school when I got together with the other guys on the football team and we would grab some communist hippie-type off the street and beat the crap out of him."

"Well, Hon, I get off work here in about fifteen minutes. The late shift is coming on duty. So I'll come over here then, and you can ask me all about the Bible. Maybe I can give you a few pointers."

Ramrod went out to the car and got his Precocious Minutes Bible. He returned to the booth and waited for her.

* * *

The next morning Bobby woke up at dawn. As soon as the first light hit the windows, Bobby was ready to make his escape. He had trained himself over the years to get up early and leave quickly and quietly, before any post-romance recriminations could get started.

Dee and Ann were still asleep, lying naked on the huge U-shaped leather couch. Bobby gathered up his clothes and changed in the kitchenette.

From there he could still see them, their bodies glistening with sweat, not to mention a few spilt beers, dried lubricants, and other things. The two women were beautiful, lying there in the naked innocence of sleep. Bobby felt a stirring in his loins, and it took a real struggle for him to leave without grabbing Ann (or Dee) and bending her over the couch just one more time.

As he walked to the front door, Bobby stopped by the video camera. It was an old type that used tapes. "No sense leaving this behind," he said as he popped the tape out of the camera and slipped it into his jacket pocket.

Reverend Bobby drove over to the church and took a quick shower in the boy's locker room, part of the Mt. Saint Mary High School. When he was finished washing off the remains of last night's encounter, he went directly to his new office at the church.

Waiting for him on the secretary's desk were eight neatly typed letters. This really made Bobby's day. Eight of the twelve members of the church's Board of Elders had resigned. Bobby was ecstatic! He could now hand pick eight new board members and solidify his control over the church. And, best of all, as he walked into his office he found another letter of resignation on his desk, this one from the Music Director. Now Bobby could hire someone with a little zip in his step. He could start playing more modern music, and not just a bunch of old hymns written by dead guys.

Bobby already knew who he wanted. His best friend in high school was a jazz musician and football prodigy, David Doom, whom Bobby and his friends called "The Doomster." It had been months since Bobby had seen him. It was time to make the call.

Bobby dialed the number. An annoyed black man, heavily laden with sleep, answered: "What?"

Bobby said, "Hi, is this the Doomster, the Doominator, the Doominatrix, the Doctor of Doom?"

"Yeah, this is David. What can I do for you?"

"Dave, this is Bobby Black. I need a Music Director."

David was a big man and his mattress was deeply dented and rutted from his body. He answered, "Gimme a minute. I'll be over," as he struggled to rise from the mattress.

The line went dead, and Bobby called his secretary into the office.

"Mary, call the four board members who didn't resign. Tell them we're having an emergency board meeting at two o'clock here at the school. Check and see if the library is available."

Mary smiled and said, "Bobby, I hope you know that I'm pulling for you. I'm sure that you're the best man to replace Reverend Bill as the Head Pastor."

"Thanks. I hope the board thinks so, too."

"And I hope you'll keep me in mind when it's time to name the new Office Manager, now that Doris is gone . . . in The Rapture."

Bobby smiled, "Sure. You know it."

As Mary turned to leave, Bobby took the VCR tape from his jacket pocket and put it in his desk drawer. "I'll watch you later on," he said to himself.

* * *

Over at the cathedral, Elder Allyson was making his own plans. He called Brother Frank and Brother Jesse into his office and laid out his idea.

"When I was talking to Reverend Black about The Rapture, I had a sudden inspiration. So I called President Nixon in New Jersey and told him my idea. Frankly, I went out on a limb. Now I have to make this work. If it goes off well, then all three of us will be installed in the big Memphis Cathedral. If it goes badly, then we may all be out in the street. Can I count on you boys to do your best?"

"Sure," the brothers chimed in.

"Okay. Here's the plan. I've been on the phone all morning and I've got it arranged so that nine retired ministers and three retired Elders are going to be flown out to Colorado. They think they're going there for a church-sponsored health care summit and retreat. In fact they are going to be permanent residents. All twelve of these men are seriously ill. Indeed, they are all near death. All twelve of them have been living in DOGGE church retirement communities. None of them have any close relatives. They were specifically chosen out of thousands of candidates.

"When they get to Pueblo tomorrow, a hospice bus will take them up into the mountains to Heaven Retirement Home, just south of Canon City. They don't know it yet, but that is where they are going to spend the rest of their lives.

"At the same time about thirty-seven ministers are flying to Pueblo. They are all scheduled to arrive tomorrow. These ministers are all men who have been accused of, let us say, 'sexual improprieties' with underage boys and girls. None of them has had criminal charges filed against them—yet. And if we succeed, none of them ever will.

"I have arranged for a bus to take them to Dodge City, Kansas, for a church centennial. As you've probably already guessed, that bus will never get to Dodge. Or at least these ministers will never get to Dodge.

Big Al pulled out his Rand McNally road atlas.

"Wednesday morning we load the ministers on the bus and start heading east from Pueblo on Highway 400. We'll stop along the way and eat lunch, and each minister will use his own credit card when he pays. When our bus gets to Nasty, Colorado, we will let the ministers off the bus to walk around at a gas station. This is so they can be seen by the locals, who will testify later that the ministers were on that bus. Then the ministers will get back on the bus. Half way between Nasty and Lamar, this bus will meet a second bus.

"Before they leave the first bus, each minister will put out a full set of clothes on the seat where he was sitting. And a pair of shoes. This will add to the 'mystery' once we reach Lamar.

"Then all the ministers will move to the second bus, which will take them back toward Pueblo. From there they will go to Heaven—the Heaven Retirement Home. Brother Frank will go with them.

"Brother Jesse and I will stay on the first bus, and when we get to Lamar we will go to the nearest church and tell them that all forty-nine ministers vanished into thin air. That's the thirty-seven ministers on the second bus, plus the twelve who are already at the retirement home. We won't use the word 'Rapture' but wait and drop hints until someone else says it. Then we can chime in, and Jesse and I will talk up The Rapture, big time.

"We will give out the names of the twelve terminally ill ministers as having been Raptured, and we'll only give out the names of the other thirty-seven ministers piecemeal, later on—after the story has dropped out of the national news.

"With any luck, we can make these problem ministers vanish, and no one will be the wiser."

"But," Frank said, "why will these thirty-seven ministers go along with your plan?"

"Some are facing criminal charges and serious jail time; all of them are facing lawsuits. The church needs this to happen because we're talking about lawsuits that could easily cost the DOGGE church over a hundred million dollars."

"Suppose you manage to make them disappear. Won't they go back to doing the stuff that got them into trouble in the first place?"

"There are no young people at the Heaven Retirement Home in Colorado. And if they do get any irrepressible urges, well, we can always send them on a short vacation to Colorado Springs or Cripple Creek. Of course we'll give them false ID's for their own protection."

"It sounds like a plan," Jesse said, knocking back a tumbler of $40-a-bottle wine.

"Yeah," Frank said. "Let's do it. It sounds just like the federal witness protection program. We can call it the PPP: the Pedophile Protection Plan!"

SEVENTEEN

David Doom arrived at Mt. Saint Mary Church and parked his old Volvo in a small corner of the lot. As he climbed out of the car, the body rose six inches, released from the weight of David's 340-pound frame.

In high school David had been a first-rate lineman. All he had to do, to stop the opponents from charging up the middle, was fall forward. His weight would flatten anyone dumb enough to stand there and take it. His football career got him a degree in Music Ed. from the university in DeKalb, but a serious ankle injury prevented David from trying out for the Chicago Bears.

Recently, David had done some teaching off and on in local high schools, and he played with a jazz band on weekends.

But David's real love was rap music.

Two years ago, David went to a talent contest and tried to break into rap. But there was a problem. David was shy in front of big crowds, and the crowd at the talent contest was enormous.

So, before he walked out onto stage, David grabbed an empty ice bucket and put it over his head. He walked out on stage and did his song, while wearing the ice bucket.

The crowd shouted "Ice Bucket! Ice Bucket! Ice Bucket!"

David "Ice Bucket" Doom was a big hit. He even won the contest. But no agents called. No one really loves a rapper named Ice Bucket. So David went back to teaching and playing a little jazz and doing a little rap for his friends each year at the Mt. Saint Mary Church Benefit and Talent Show. Some days David wished his name really was Ice Bucket, rather than The Doomster.

But on this Monday morning, David was "called" to be Music Director. He met Bobby Black at the door and both men went into the two o'clock meeting of the board. As they walked into the school library, David noticed the four Elders and the church secretary already sitting at the big conference table in the center of the room. These four men would be the ones to decide if he would get on the church payroll. But with Bobby's help and recommendation, David felt like it was a sure thing.

Bobby stepped up to the table. "Well, gentlemen, I guess we all know why we're here."

"Yeah, Bobby," Moe the car salesman said, "we have some serious business to deal with. But it looks like we don't have a quorum."

"Mary, don't write that in the minutes," Bobby said. "Now listen, Moe, these problems have to be dealt with today. We can't put this off. And so I'm going to pass on some wisdom from the Reverend Doctor Bill Eous. He told me once, 'As long as no one raises the issue of whether or not you have a quorum, then it's not really an issue—if you get my drift.' Besides, Moe, you know that this board has taken action many times in the past without having a quorum."

"Okay, well if you think it's that important, Bobby, let's go ahead."

Larry the funeral director and Curly the insurance agent chimed in, "Yep, let's do this."

Shemp, who was the Principal of Mt. Saint Mary School, nodded his head vigorously, like he was a bobble-head doll.

Of course, all the board members did a lot of business through and for the church, and they depended on the good will of the Head Pastor.

"Don't get me wrong," Moe said. "I just want to make sure no one comes back later and questions our decisions. We don't want that."

Larry and Curly nodded their heads vigorously. Shemp was unsure about showing any reaction at all, at least until he could get a better sense of which way the wind was blowing.

"Hey, don't worry about it. I'll get together with Mary later and make sure the minutes of this meeting all look on the up and up."

"Okay, then let's go ahead," Moe said.

"First of all, I've looked over the Church Rule, and it says that when you have a resignation from the Board, the rest of the Board can continue to do business as long as you have two-thirds of the remaining members. Here in my hand I have eight letters of resignation from Board members." Bobby smiled and surveyed the faces at the table.

"Well, would anyone move that we accept these resignations?"

"I so move," said Shemp.

"I second," said Larry.

"All in agreement?" Moe said. All four hands shot up.

"Okay, great!" Bobby said. "This means that you four now represent 100% of the remaining Board members. Any decision you make today will carry the full force of an official Board decision. And the first thing we need to look at is the question of replacing Reverend Bill in the job of Head Pastor."

This announcement was followed by a considerable amount of shifting chairs and sidelong glances.

"First of all," Bobby continued. "I want all of you to know that, if you allow me to serve as Head Pastor, I would be glad to do so at my current salary."

This stunning offer caught the board off guard.

"Well, Bobby, sure. If that's what you want," Moe said. The others, impressed with Bobby's generous offer, nodded their heads quickly.

"Okay then. Does someone want to move that I be named the new Head Pastor?"

"I so move," said Shemp.

"I second," said Larry.

"All in agreement?" Moe said. All four hands shot up.

"Okay, great!" Bobby said. "I want to let you know that Elder Allyson Smith has kindly recommended a man to replace me as Assistant Minister. But we have time to go into that later. The next order of business is replacing the Office Manager, Doris Morris. Does anyone have any objection to my naming Mary, here, as the new Office Manager?"

"That sounds fine," Moe said.

"Good. We also have a resignation letter from the former Music Director. Does anyone have an objection to hiring Brother David here as the new Music Director?"

"We all know David," Shemp said. "I'm sure he would be fine. Perhaps we could hire him on a six-month contract and see how he works out."

"Sounds fine," Moe said.

"Good, good," Bobby said. "Then we're all in agreement?"

Heads nodded vigorously.

"Well then, Mary, let the record show that these decisions were made by a unanimous vote of the board."

Mary, newly raised to the job of Office Manager, was only too happy to add this in her minutes.

"Now there are two more issues that we have to deal with. And these are perhaps the most difficult. In talking with Elder Allyson Smith, I've learned that the DOGG Evangelical Church wants to sever its formal ties with Mt. Saint Mary Church."

There was a look of concern on all four faces.

"I've given this a lot of thought. I've prayed over it and prayed over it. And I agree with Elder Allyson. This church is growing fast, and we need the freedom to develop and expand without having to turn to the church hierarchy for permission. Frankly, Elder Allyson told me that he feels we need to be able to go about doing God's Work, without unnecessary interference from the New Jersey headquarters. We would, of course, continue working with school accreditation bodies and supporting the church's mission work, but in fact from now on we would be only loosely affiliated with the larger DOGGE Church."

Moe was nodding his head, while Principal Shemp smiled and shifted in his chair.

"So, anyway, I feel that we need to vote on this. I would like a motion that would establish and incorporate this church as a free and independent body—the New Rapture Church of Mt. Saint Mary, Illinois."

"I so move," said Shemp.

"I second," said Larry.

"All in agreement?" Moe said. All four hands shot up.

"Okay, great!" Bobby said, smiling. "And now there is only one last problem. As you know, the church has been providing videos of Reverend Bill's Message on The Rapture to people through our church website. Honestly, the time and expense of this task has proven to be a real burden on Mary and our volunteer staff. Something needs to be done to shift the work and the expense of producing and mailing out these tapes to someone else."

All four men were nodding and smiling.

"Anyway, I've arranged with a small distribution company here in Chicago to take over this task. This company is creating a new division called 'New Rapture Tapes and DVDs, Inc.' and it will pay our church a token payment of $1 to take over the production and distribution of the tapes. We will probably continue to offer volunteers to help with the work, and this company will set up shop in the parsonage across the street."

"But Bobby," Moe said, "as Head Pastor, that parsonage is your home. You shouldn't have to give it up."

"Thanks, Moe. I understand your concern. And I certainly appreciate it. But let me say this: Making these videos available to others is Reverend Bill's great legacy. Now that he is taken up in The Rapture, it is all that we have left of him. It's his gift to all of God's children. I'm more than happy to turn over that house to them. It's more important that Reverend Bill's legacy of love and hope continue. I can stay in my apartment. It's not like I have a wife and children to support. I can continue to 'bach' it in my apartment across town."

"Jeez, Bobby, that's a lot to give up. I'm sure we all appreciate what you're doing here, how much you're sacrificing to do God's Work and promote His church."

"Don't give it a second thought."

"Well, at least we should talk about a housing stipend to help you pay your rent."

"Thanks, Moe, we can go into that some other time."

"Fine, Bobby."

"So what I would like to suggest is that we vote on this."

Brother Shemp started to raise his hand.

"Just a minute," Bobby said. "I have a letter of agreement here which I'd like you to look at. Here are copies." Bobby passed out the papers. "Now this document transfers ownership of the tapes made by Reverend Bill to this company 'New Rapture Tapes and DVDs, Inc.' for the price of one dollar. In addition, the company will agree to rent the parsonage on a month-to-month lease and use that space to produce and distribute the tapes."

"You mean," Shemp said, "the company is going to pay us rent for the parsonage?"

"That's right. This company is a God-friendly company that wants to help us do God's Work. It's only right that they pay us for using this space."

"That's very generous of them."

"I agree. But that's the way they want it. So do I hear a motion to accept this offer?"

"I so move," said Shemp.

"I second," said Larry.

"All in agreement?" Moe asked. All four hands shot up.

"Okay, great!" Bobby said, smiling. "I'll pass the letter of agreement around, and each of you can sign it and date it. Mary will notarize it later."

As each of the men took a few seconds to glance over the agreement and sign his name, Bobby wondered if they would be so quick to sell the tapes if they knew that the actual owner of New Rapture Tapes and DVDs, Inc., was, in fact, Reverend Bobby B. Black. And, as sole owner of the tapes, Rev. Bobby Black now stood to make a fortune selling tapes of Reverend Bill Eous—the soon-to-be world famous minister who was taken up in The Rapture. Luckily Reverend Bill was long gone, having stolen $375,000 in church funds—not to mention a church secretary—and was in no position to complain.

Each of the four board members signed the letter, and Bobby passed it to Mary.

"That covers the business I wanted to get done today. Is there any other business the board wishes to address?"

Bobby waited for a few seconds. "I call this meeting adjourned."

The board members shook hands and slowly made their way out to the parking lot. David held back.

"Bobby, what do I need to do?"

"Well, you have a whole day to work on the music for Wednesday night. You probably ought to talk to the school principal about your teaching duties there, too."

"Okay, great!" David shifted out of his chair and headed out the door. Now only Mary was left behind, waiting for her chance to talk to Bobby. From the look on her face, he knew that this was going to be his toughest sell of the day.

Before she could speak, Bobby said, "Mary, why don't you get some volunteers and start taking Reverend Bill's stuff out of the parsonage. But, why don't you go over there, first, and see if there's anything you want for yourself. I mean, most of the living room furniture will have to stay, but you should certainly get a memento to help you remember Reverend Bill. Maybe the big television or the stereo set, or even that nice antique bedroom set upstairs."

Mary looked confused.

"Okay, Bobby. But we need to talk sometime soon."

EIGHTEEN

When Ramrod Steel woke up Monday morning, his head hurt and his "John Thomas" was aching so badly that he thought he had slammed it in the car door. But then he remembered last night.

After the waitress came back to his booth in the IHOP, Ramrod talked to her for a long time about the Bible, and The Rapture, and God's plan for His people to survive The Tribulation.

The waitress—he thought her name was Missy Duncan—sat next to him and listened intently to every word he said. No one had paid this much attention to Ramrod in a long, long time, and he was absolutely sure that Missy was responding to the Eternal Truth and Verity of God's Word.

Ramrod's mind was flush with a thousand different ideas. Soon the ideas were flowing and mixing, and the feeling of Missy sitting up close to him in the booth, it was just so overwhelming. His feelings all seemed to jumble together. God's love was mixed in with the more human variety, and the next thing you know Ramrod and Missy were in the Ladies Room, and Ramrod was pressed against the door, as Missy gave him the most exquisite blowjob he had ever had in his life.

The memories of last night slowly moved through Ramrod's mind, like molasses out of a mole's ass, and soon Ramrod began to worry about the burning sensation he was feeling "down below."

Worse yet, as he sat up, Ramrod saw a naked woman stretched face-down across the foot of his bed. It was Missy.

Ramrod whispered, under his breath, "Damn! Where is The Rapture when you really need it?"

* * *

Monday morning Brother John Doyle drove from the alcohol rehab center in Beaver Dam, Wisconsin, to the suburbs of Chicago. He had gotten "the call" that morning. Elder Allyson Smith told him that he was now Assistant Pastor at the New Rapture Church.

"From now on you'll be working for Reverend Bobby Black."

Brother John thanked Big Al profusely.

Big Al said, "I had to pull a lot of strings and cash in a lot of favors to get you this gig. SO DON'T SCREW IT UP!"

John tried to thank Big Al one more time, but the phone went dead.

Brother John Doyle was an ex-Marine, going on fifty-five years old. He was built like a fire-plug and sported a traditional Marine haircut. And he was a man who was pretty much all worn out and used up.

Years ago, while in the Marines and stationed in Japan, Corporal John Doyle had learned how to drink Sakae. And like he did with most other alcoholic things, he got very good at it. John also developed a taste for youngish-looking Japanese girls, a taste that he shared with some of his Marine friends. The mix of alcohol and Japanese schoolgirls occasionally got him into serious hot water.

After leaving the Marines, John's problem with drinking led him to AA, but it didn't do much to cut his taste for booze. Brother John tried juggling booze and God, but he always dropped the ball with one or the other. Brother John tried going to a seminary, but he flunked out. And so he became a traveling evangelist.

After twenty years of working the "Revival" circuit in the South and Southwest, Brother John had almost nothing to show for his life. He had an ex in Texas and two grown children who never spoke to him or returned his phone calls. It was like he just never could catch a decent break.

But what really bothered him was that one of his drinking buddies—a guy who was even more obsessed with Japanese schoolgirls than he was—why, this guy was now a famous television evangelist! It was like—Hey! there's no goddamn justice in this world.

Brother John hoped this new job at the Mt. Saint Mary Church would finally be the break he needed. It could be a new beginning. It could be a turning point, a renewal of faith and purpose, a first step toward redemption for all the stupid and hurtful things he had done in his life. It could be a new birth in spirit and hope and joy.

While he was on his way to the church, John saw a strip club near the off-ramp and a big sign that said:

MR. BENNIE HAN'S EXOTIC ASIAN GIRLS

Brother John figured that, what the hell, God could wait one more day. Or two.

* * *

Ramrod Steel slipped on his housecoat and wandered downstairs. Unfortunately, Cloye chose that moment to walk into her parents' bedroom looking for her wayward father. Instead she found Missy Duncan lying on the bed, a sheet draped across her naked body.

"Oh, Christ!" Cloye said. "You'd think he could keep it in his pants for more than ten days."

Cloye sat on the bed next to Missy and pushed her—well, actually she shoved her—four or five times until Missy woke up.

"Who are you?" Cloye said, in as stern a voice as she could manage.

"Huh? Oh, you must by Ramrod's daughter Cloye. I'm a friend of your father."

"I guessed that much. So why don't you get your clothes on. It's time to go."

Missy covered her face with her hands and she began to tear up.

"Now don't start that with me!" Cloye said. "You've had your fun and now it's time to get going."

"I . . . I'm sorry. I never meant for it to be this way. It's just, I know so much about your father and you, from all the times I talked to your mother."

"You're a friend of Mom's?"

"Well, sort of. She used to come into the IHOP where I work."

"So, you're a waitress?"

"Yeah. Actually I work two shifts: one at IHOP and a second job at Wal-Mart. I'm trying to save enough money for my next surgery."

"Okay. I'll bite. What surgery?"

"Well, I probably shouldn't tell you this. My name is Missy . . . Melissa. But five years ago my legal name wasn't Melissa. It was Melvin."

"Oh great, this is really the icing on the cake! You're a tranny. And when were you going to tell Dad this?"

"Well, I didn't get around to telling him last night. But I really like your Dad. I think we hit it off together."

"Yeah, that's right Mr. Obvious. You have everything he's looking for in a woman."

"Why . . . thanks."

Cloye sat quietly on the bed. What could she do?

"Okay, I'll keep your secret for now. But you have to tell him the truth, and soon."

"I will. I will. I like your dad and he likes me. He already told me he wants to take me to church with him on Wednesday night."

"Really? Have you ever been to this church before?"

"No. But I'm sure it's nice."

Cloye got up and left the bedroom, As she walked down the hall, past Ireme's display cabinet, the too-large eyes of the Precocious Minutes figurines seemed to follower her.

* * *

Rev. Bobby managed to put off talking to Mary until Tuesday morning.

At ten o'clock Mary brought Bobby a pot of coffee on a sterling silver tray, and she sat down in the plush leather chair in front of his new desk.

"Is there something you want, Mary?"

"Well, yes, Bobby, there is. I'm a little worried about this deal with the videos."

"The Rapture videos? What about them."

"As you know the church website has sold over $52,000 in videos, just during the last week."

"Yes. But keep in mind that those were 'love offerings,' not sales. What about it?"

"Well, Bobby, don't take this the wrong way, but I'm not sure that the church should sell the rights to all those videos for a dollar."

"I understand your concern, but frankly the church just can't handle that volume of business. What do you think we should do?"

"I don't know. But I think the church should be getting more than a lousy dollar for all those videos Reverend Bill made over the years."

"So. You think we're making a business mistake."

"I do."

"You know, once New Rapture Tapes and DVDs gets off the ground, they're going to need someone to run the operation on a day-to-day basis. I think you would be a good person to run the company, maybe even as an Executive Vice President. You would be making a lot more money than you could ever make here as Office Manager."

"That would be wonderful. But why do you think they would hire me?"

"I know the owner. I can pretty much guarantee that you would get the job."

Mary sat in her chair, quietly, thinking it over.

"That sounds great. But I think I really need to talk to the church board about this."

"That's fine, Mary, but there is something else you and I need to discuss first. I was talking to the groundskeeper this morning and he said that the stereo system is missing from the parsonage."

Mary's eyes opened wide.

"But, Bobby, you told me I could take the stereo as a memento of Reverend Bill!"

"I did? I don't seem to remember saying that. Besides, I don't have the right to dispose of Reverend Bill's personal property. That stereo was worth at least $3,500. And whoever took it is guilty of grand larceny." Bobby paused to let it sink in. "It would be a shame, a crying shame for someone to lose her job just because of a little mistake. Of course, I always try to practice forgiveness for the sins of others."

Mary squirmed in her chair.

"But, on the other hand, I'm sure the church board would frown on someone taking advantage of Reverend Bill's 'disappearance' to go through the parsonage and steal his stuff. They would almost certainly want to call in the police and demand that the thief be punished to the full extent of the law."

"Wait a minute," Mary said. "I just figured it out! *You're* the owner of New Rapture Tapes!"

Bobby laughed. "That's ridiculous. And it would be almost impossible to prove."

"This whole thing, it's just a trick so you can get the money from those videos."

"Mary, that's an absurd accusation, and I'm terribly offended. You shouldn't be trying to make this about me!"

"I know now what you're up to."

"I think, Mary, what we have here is called a Mexican standoff. On the one hand, if you press the issue, you might be able to get me fired from the pastor's job. But that's not a sure thing. Besides I already have legal possession of the videos." Bobby let the situation sink in. "On the other hand, I can accuse you of stealing the stereo, and at the very least I can get you fired from your job as Office Manager. You might even end up doing some jail time."

Bobby stood up and began pacing back and forth, the same way Reverend Bill used to when he had to make a tough decision. "Why don't we try looking at this situation from a God-centered perspective. Suppose we start accusing each other of this stuff. Pretty soon the police will be involved. At the very least the District Attorney will want to audit the church books, and you and I both know that a criminal investigation would destroy this church." Bobby stopped short and faced Mary.

"Do you want to destroy this church?"

"No."

"Good, then let's let things just go on the way they are. And I'll forget about the stereo."

Mary sat quietly for several minutes.

"What will happen when people notice that the money isn't coming in from the video sales anymore? There will be questions."

"So what would you suggest?"

"I suppose you could divide sales between the in-state sales and the out-of-state sales. The in-state sales could be run through the church so there wouldn't be any sales tax. The out-of-state sales from the website could go through New Rapture, since there wouldn't be any sales tax that way, either. We could ask a flat $19.95 per tape, plus shipping, and divide the orders between the church and New Rapture, as they come in."

"That's brilliant. Now I know why you would make a great Executive V.P.!"

"And New Rapture, could still charge the church $18.95 a tape for duplication costs. The church would make a dollar a tape, more if volunteers do the packing and shipping."

"Fantastic! Mary, you're a genius."

"No one at the church would ever suspect why the church makes so little money off the tapes. Almost all the profits would end up with New Rapture."

"Why don't you get on that right now. Our computer guy can write a program for the web site to sort the incoming orders by state."

Mary left, carrying the sterling silver tray.

Bobby said to himself, "Gee, I wonder if Reverend Bill ever tried to put the make on Mary? She really is something else. She's amazing! Even if she is kinda plain." And then he began opening his desk drawers—as if looking for something—and said, "Reverend Bill must have kept a paper bag around here someplace."

NINETEEN

A few days after Dubyah narrowly escaped the "assassination plot," Mark heard on state television that the Texrectumstanian Secret Police had rounded up two dozen leaders of the Full Moon Party. According to the television report, a group of protesters were complaining about the arrests and a pro-Full Moon rally was planned for that afternoon at the city's main park.

When Mark arrived by taxi, he was surprised. There were no protestors anywhere in sight. The park was almost empty.

Mark got out of the taxi and asked people where the protest was. No one wanted to talk to him, much less answer questions about Dubyah's enemies. Finally a British reporter arrived on the scene, and he recognized Mark.

"Where are the protesters?"

"Ahhh, the protesters," the Brit said, as he nodded his head politely.

"Yeah, where are they?"

"Those blokes were taken to the 'official protest area'—I would guess."

"And where is that?"

"It's about fifty miles out of town, in the middle of an abandoned nuclear facility. The police carted them away hours ago. By now the protesters are probably growing third eyes and extra fingers."

Mark suddenly decided that, by God, he was going to find some protesters. But maybe some who were not so far away. Maybe there were some here in town.

Half an hour later, Mark found his way to the maximum security prison where the Full Moon Party leaders were being held and severely "questioned." As his taxi pulled up, he saw a group of Full Moon Party members gathered around the prison. And they were actually chanting slogans—in English! Mark pulled out his video camera and focused on the protesters.

A group of Full Moon Party members were clearly angry and critical of Dubyah and the Half Moon Party. They held up signs and chanted:

"Bigger cages, longer chains! Bigger cages, longer chains! Bigger cages, longer chains!"

Deep down in his heart of hearts, Mark knew that Nickelay's government wouldn't hold up long under this kind of intense criticism.

* * *

Tuesday morning Big Al, along with Brothers Jesse and Frank, arrived at the airport in Pueblo, Colorado. Big Al spent most of the day calling some of his associates, including an old friend in Colorado Springs. Then he went to bed. Meanwhile, Jesse and Frank were greeting the ministers at the airport and making sure they got to their hotel rooms. It was important to make sure that all thirty-seven ministers arrived in good order and were safely tucked away. The last thing they needed was for some of these horny old goats to wander off in dowtown Pueblo, looking for a good time with some teenagers.

Wednesday morning their bus was waiting outside the hotel. Big Al, Frank, and Jesse got the ministers organized and piled them into the bus. Jesse had some experience driving big rigs, so he was going to drive the bus from Pueblo to Dodge City. One of the ministers had experience driving school buses, and Big Al planned for him to drive the second bus, which was already stashed behind an abandoned gas station between Nasty, Colorado, and Lamar.

Big Al was pleased with how well his plan was working.

Heading east from the airport they soon found themselves in some of the most desolate territory in the central plains. There were a few cows, scattered here and there, and some horses, but not much else. The ministers seemed a bit uneasy because Elder Allyson didn't bother to explain his plan. All they knew was that they were about to go into hiding.

After about forty-five miles traveling due east, the bus stopped for lunch at a greasy spoon. Big Al made sure it took credit cards before letting the ministers order. According to plan, each minister paid with his own card in order to establish an electronic paper trail.

After another fifty miles, they stopped at the gas station in Nasty, Colorado, and the ministers got out to stretch their legs and use the toilet—but mainly so they would be seen by the locals.

They piled back on the bus, and Jesse drove east to where the second bus was waiting. He parked out of sight, behind the abandoned gas station. There each of the ministers laid out a set of clothes—shirt, shorts, socks, pants—on his seat on the bus and then got off. Jesse, Frank, and Big Al put out the additional twelve sets of clothes to represent the terminally ill ministers. These twelve were already on their way west on the hospice bus, going up into the mountains toward Canon City.

Brother Frank and the ministers transferred to the second bus and took off back west, toward Pueblo. Big Al wanted them to get a good head start toward Canon City and the retirement home. No point taking chances.

Once the bus was well on its way, Big Al and Brother Jesse drove the bus east to Lamar. It was time for Big Al's ready-made Rapture to take place.

* * *

Reverend Bobby enjoyed the moment. He was now on the road to fame and fortune. He could run the New Rapture Church and milk it for every cent he could get. At the same time his new company New Rapture Tapes and DVDs, Inc. would be making a ton of money.

There was a knock. Bobby opened the solid oak door and found standing there a rough and disheveled man, with a pasty color, red eyes and the smell of alcohol on him. He looked like hell.

"Are you Reverend Bobby?"

"Yes."

"I'm Brother John Doyle. I think Elder Allyson told you about me."

"Ah, yes. Brother John. I remember Elder Allyson mentioning that you would be coming. I'm surprised you got here so fast."

"I was in rehab—but I guess he told you that—I was stuck up in Beaver Dam, Wisconsin. It's not that far a drive. I've had a serious problem with alcohol."

"Really?"

"I've struggled with Demon Rum for most of my life. But I'm much better now."

"I see. Well, if your drink is rum, I don't suppose you would want a shot of whiskey, now, would you?" Bobby opened his desk drawer and pulled out a bottle. "This belonged to Reverend Eous before he got raptured."

"Since you're having one, I guess I could use a shot. Just to steady my nerves."

Bobby poured the booze into two paper cups. "Sorry about the cups, I still haven't found where Reverend Bill kept the good crystal."

"That's fine, thanks!" John said as he took the cup in his trembling hands.

Bobby took a sip of whiskey; then he leaned back in his plush office chair and stared for a while at his new protégé.

"Listen, John, I think you're not the kind of guy who stays around one place very much, are you?"

"What do you mean?"

"It's just my impression that you've done a lot of traveling. You've been on the evangelistic bandwagon for a lot of years. Am I right?"

"Yeah. It's what destroyed my marriage."

"I can imagine. But you're not really a one-woman guy anyway, are you?"

"Son, I was in the Marines for six years. And I spent a lot of time in South-East Asia."

"Vietnam?"

"Well, actually I was in Korea and Japan most of the time."

"And what did you do after that?"

"The Marines gave me some training in bookkeeping. So after I got out I found a job with the IRS."

"You were an IRS agent?"

"Sure, for five years. I worked in downtown Cincinnati, mostly collecting back taxes from bars and small shops. But eventually the booze caught up with me. Then I found AA and I found God. I went to seminary for a while, but I couldn't quite see eye to eye with my teachers.

Then I paired up with an old evangelist called Brother Jim, and we did a lot of traveling and preaching—and a lot of drinking and whoring around. Especially in those Texas border towns. But God always forgave me afterwards. For the past few years I've been doing a little evangelistic work for Elder Allyson."

"It sounds like you have some interesting skills. Maybe you could take a look at the church books. I've had a guy named Andy Arthur going over them, and he's cleaned up a lot of problems. But it wouldn't hurt to have someone with your training go over the books, just to see what you can do."

"Sure. I can do that."

"I suppose you've heard about how things are changing here at New Rapture Church. We're going off in a whole new direction. And people are responding! This is the fastest growing church in Chicago, and probably the whole Midwest."

"I'll be glad to do anything I can to help."

"I'll probably send you off to several cities to start new churches that teach the New Rapture theology. There are a lot of franchise opportunities. We have a real growth potential. And you're just the kind of guy I want to have in on the ground floor."

Bobby poured John another shot of whiskey.

"Johnny, I don't really see you as the typical Assistant Pastor type. You'd probably get bored to death visiting the sick or trying to run a Sunday school. Am I right?"

"Yeah, I guess so."

"Hey, that's fine. I've got plenty of people to do that kind of stuff for me. What I need is someone who knows how to preach the Hell out of people. I want to be able to send you to Rockford, or Peoria, or Indianapolis and know that, by God, you're gonna save a bunch of people from Damnation. You're gonna lead them to Christ, come hell or high water."

"I'm your man."

"And even more than that, I need someone who can watch my back. And . . . let's just suppose a couple of guys came over to the church and tried to twist my arm. I think you're the kind of guy who would jump in and kick ass. Am I right?"

"Look, Bobby. Let me be straight with you. You give me this chance, and I'll kill any mutherfucker who tries to lay a hand on you."

"Or two mutherfuckers."

"Two, three, five … hell, bring 'em on."

"Great! So if some thug comes to the church and tries to break my arm, I can count on you to bust a cap in his ass?"

"Yeah . . . well . . . I guess. Whatever that means."

Bobby smiled and said, "So why don't you go see my secretary. She'll cut you a check for let's say $2,000 so you can get an apartment and clothes and food."

"To be honest, Bobby, I don't need an apartment. I'm on the road so much, I usually just live out of the Y."

"Okay, that sounds fine. So let me start making some calls and by next month we should have you out on the road. Does that sound okay to you?"

"Great."

"In the mean time, I want you to watch the DVD of my sermon last Sunday. You'll need to start thinking about how you can bring this 'New Rapture' idea into your sermons, too. Also, maybe we should plan on you preaching next Wednesday night, just so people can meet you."

"I'm just like an old fire horse. All I need is the smell of Smoke and Hellfire and I'm ready to charge in and preach the damnedest sermon you ever heard."

"I believe it."

Bobby poured another round and thought about the bounty of God's Providence in bringing to his door just the man he needed to transform the New Rapture Church into Bobby's own little kingdom on earth.

TWENTY

Late Wednesday afternoon a single bus pulled into the drive of the DOGG Evangelical Church in Lamar, Colorado. It was a small church, but there were a few people around—mainly elderly women who were attending a quilting party at the church's education center.

Brother Jesse climbed down from the bus and ran to the women, yelling, "They're gone! They're all gone!"

The women were frightened at first. Mrs. Stella Johnson-Freese thought he was yelling about the condoms being missing from the bus's first-aid kit. It took a few minutes before she realized that Brother Jesse was yelling about people who were missing.

"The ministers on the bus. We were driving down the highway, and they all just disappeared!"

"That's right," Elder Allyson added as he caught up with Jesse. "There were forty-nine ministers on that bus. But they vanished into thin air."

"It was horrible! Horrible!" Jesse shrieked, as he badly overacted his part. Elder Allyson had coached Jesse for a solid hour on what to say, but here he was ad libbing. Al winced as Jesse stumbled over his lines and began to pantomime an invisible man eating a visible sandwich. But as an all-too-visible man eating an invisible sandwich, Jesse couldn't get the idea across to his audience. They just didn't get it.

"He was eatin' a sandwich, and he disappeared!" Jesse wailed.

The police arrived, and minutes later a reporter from the newspaper and a local radio jock showed up at the church. Al told the story over again, about how the whole busload of ministers had slowly evaporated into thin air.

Soon the crowd got bigger and bigger. When the journalists asked who was on the bus, Elder Allyson kept repeating the names of the twelve terminally ill ministers who, at that moment, were enjoying the hot tubs, shuffleboard courts, and massage parlors of the newly renamed Heaven Retirement Home.

And every time a reporter asked, "Where do you think the ministers are right now?" Big Al would answer, "I'm sure they're in Heaven!"

* * *

Mark sent the video of the anti-Dubyah demonstration to the *Weekly Whirled News* office in Moscow. They would send it by satellite to the main office in New York. Meanwhile Mark returned to his hotel room to work on the story of the attempted assassination of Dubyah and the protests of the Full Moon Party.

But just as Mark sat down, the phone rang and a mysterious voice said, "Mark, you remember me? If you recognize my voice, do not say my name. Your phone is probably bugged. Just meet me at the library across the street in five minutes. Make sure you're not followed."

The message was followed by a click and then a second audible click as the Secret Police hung up their phone tap. A government agent was immediately dispatched to the library across the street from Mark's hotel, but there was no library. There was only a Turkish coffee bar and a Sudanese laundry. So the agent went back to the office to get new orders.

In the mean time, Mark walked across the street to the coffee bar and looked for the mysterious caller. Mark was sure he would be sitting at a table in the back.

And, sure enough, Mark saw a strange man sitting in a booth, far back in the darkest corner of the bar. He was wearing a worn black suit and a fake moustache. The thick plastic glasses were also obviously phony. Mark realized that the caller must be British, as only a Brit would wear such a stupid looking disguise.

"Mark! Over here," the gentleman caller loudly whispered, while trying to look inconspicuous.

Mark paid for a cup of steaming, black, nasty-tasting liquid that couldn't pass for coffee anywhere else in the civilized world, except perhaps in Starbucks. The smell of the stuff was so revolting that Mark struggled to keep from vomiting. He made a bitter face as he sat down in the booth. The stranger said, "I know it tastes horrible, but it's the most popular drink they have. You see what people are reduced to when they can't have alcohol."

The face was barely visible under the fake moustache, but the voice was familiar.

"Dick! It's you!"

"Shhhh! Not so loud. I'm supposed to be dead you know."

"But I saw your car explode. I saw you sitting in the car."

"Oh, that wasn't me. That was a car thief. He was leaning forward to hot wire the ignition when the bomb under the seat went off."

"But weren't you standing near the car when it exploded?"

"Not that close. Actually I was pissing on the tire of a brand new Mercedes. It's what I do when I've had too much to drink. I look for expensive cars and piss on the tires. Generally I prefer a German or Italian make, but French cars are nice, too."

"I guess you're lucky to be alive."

"It takes more than a bomb to get rid of Dick the Welshman!"

"But what are you doing in Texrectumstan?"

"I'm following up on an international plot of such enormous proportions—well, you just wouldn't believe it. It's gigantic!"

"Well, maybe I would believe it. What's it about?"

"I've heard rumors that Dubyah the Younger is planning to attack Iraq shortly after he takes office as Fearless Leader. Dubyah plans to justify the attack based on secret intelligence that Iraq has nuclear weapons and plans to use them against Texrectumstan."

"Does Iraq have nuclear weapons?"

"No one seriously believes that, but Nickelay Dubyah wants to start a war with Iraq, and he really doesn't care if the information is true or not."

"Where is he getting this secret intelligence?"

"There are dozens of forged documents created and paid for by the English financier, Jonathan Seagull, and a secretive group of Italian bankers. Evidently, the American industrialist, Todd Fox-Halburton, arranged dozens of shipments of metal tubes to be sent to Iraq, knowing that foreign agents would suspect the development of nuclear capabilities. Both Seagull and Fox-Halburton are feeding false information to the Secret Police of Texrectumstan."

"So why does Dubyah want to start a war with Iraq. Is he after the oil?"

"Not really, though the opportunity to seize the oil fields is a nice bonus."

"Then what is he after?"

"He knows that the economy of Texrectumstan is on the skids. Millions of manufacturing jobs have moved to other countries. Most of the country's farms and forests, its mines and factories, and even its telecommunications and banking system are now under the control of international corporations. The whole country is essentially bankrupt, and most people don't even know it! During the reign of Nickelay the Elder, these international corporations were given a free hand to grab everything they could and run. And now there's almost nothing left."

"So what is Dubyah the Younger going to do?"

"Dubyah and his friends are going to make one last grab to get everything that isn't nailed down. It's like the American savings and loan scandals all over again. It's just like Enron. The leaders are going to raid the cookie jar one last time before the whole thing collapses."

"But if they've already taken everything, then why start a war?"

"First of all it distracts people from what's really going on. The news media focus on the war and not on the massive theft going on under their very noses. And since the news media is essentially owned and controlled by the international corporations, it's not hard to get them to look the other way."

"And when the war is over?"

"That's just it. The war will never be over. Once Iraq is defeated, then Dubyah will look for new enemies. He'll pick fights with other countries, maybe even start some kind of holy war against the infidels. And as long as the war is going on, he'll keep getting re-elected as Fearless Leader."

"And I guess that as long as he is Fearless Leader, there's no chance that any of his crooked friends will go to jail."

"Right. Dubyah wants to stay in office as long as he can, to keep the police from investigating his friends, and to hide the truth about what he's doing."

Mark thought about this for a while, wondering what he—as a member of the Media Elite—could do to stop Dubyah's monstrous plan. But then Mark remembered that he had just made a down payment to buy a townhouse in Chicago. And suddenly the idea of going after Dubyah and his cronies didn't seem quite so important.

WEDNESDAY AFTERNOON Reverend Bobby Black heard the strange news coming out of Colorado. A group of DOGGE ministers had been taken up in The Rapture, or at least that was the story that was making the rounds on the cable news channels. Bobby wasn't at all surprised to find out that Big Al and Brother Jesse were in the bus when the ministers got raptured. Bobby could smell something fishy from as far away as Chicago.

Bobby didn't know what Elder Allyson was up to, and frankly he didn't care. All that he knew for sure was that this new disappearance was going to help New Rapture Church a lot. He quickly got on the phone and warned his staff to expect a big crowd. They would have to set up more loudspeakers outside the church. The New Rapture Church could hold over fifteen hundred souls, but Bobby was sure twice that many would show up tonight, especially once the local television stations started to connect the Rapture in Colorado with the Rapture of Reverend Bill Eous, and Mrs. Ramrod Steel and her son. Not to mention (and he would rather not) the raptured church secretary, Mrs. Doris Morris.

Bobby personally supervised the setting up of the cameras and the testing of the loudspeakers. He took a blank tape from his desk and loaded it into the system's recorder himself. Reverend Bobby was a hands-on type of leader, and the sermon he was going to preach tonight—well it was going to be a barn burner.

Suddenly, Bobby stopped. In that instant, he came to a full and complete stop, as if he had run into a wall. He looked at the tape in his hand, then at the camera. He said, "Now I can sell videos of my own sermons on the website, along with the old tapes and DVDs of Reverend Bill!" At that moment the future looked particularly bright. With a little hard work, New Rapture Tapes and DVDs, Inc. could become a major player in the world of Christian media. Bobby pictured millions and millions of dollars. *His* dollars.

Bobby felt an electric charge go through his body. He knew that this must be the same kind of feeling that Oral Roberts had that day, years ago, when he realized that he could through the force of his own will (and the help of God, Almighty) build the biggest church in Tulsa and start a television ministry, and maybe even build his own university, Oral U. It would take hard work, but Bobby Black's New Rapture Church could one day become a light shining on a hill, for all the world to see and admire.

WEDNESDAY MORNING Ireme Steel woke Doray up and got him dressed and ready. It seemed strange not to have to worry about Ramrod. He was so disorganized around the house. Was he eating? How was the laundry getting done? But Ireme understood that these problems were not her problems, at least not anymore. She had left Ramrod. She had no choice. Ramrod's secular view of the world was having a bad influence on Doray. And it was getting harder and harder for Ireme to hold true to her own beliefs and still live in a household where religion was treated like a hobby with no connection to anything else.

Today was Employees-Get-in-Free Day, and Ireme wanted to show Doray the wonders of the Precocious Minutes Theme Park. The gates at PMTP opened promptly at 9:00 a.m., and Ireme wanted to enjoy every precocious minute of their day at the park.

The city bus took Ireme and Doray west out of town, along hills filled with lush vegetation—the (nearly) unspoiled beauty of the Missouri Ozarks. The dozens of theaters and fast food restaurants seemed like blemishes on the green hills. Soon, the bus pulled into the long drive at Precocious Minutes Theme Park, which included plenty of convenient parking for RVs and tourist buses.

Ireme led Doray to the magnificent entrance. At the gateway was a fountain with three large brass sculptures lining the pool. Each figure was a different Precocious Minutes Angel, the soft lines of their features matching the enormous bulbous heads and the dwarfish bodies. The brightly colored waters jetted from the brass sculptures in ways that naturally reinforced a belief in the miraculous.

Next to the entrance was a small theater where they showed a short biographic film of Mr. Frank Slaughter, Jr., the founder of PMTP. The short film covered the more important facts of Mr. Slaughter's life and his vision for Precocious Minutes Theme Park.

Mr. Slaughter was the last of twelve children of Frank Slaughter, Sr., who had owned a pig farm outside St. Louis. His father's father had been a sculptor who worked for the biggest mausoleum in Saint Louis. Frank Jr. learned about art by copying pictures from Bible story books and coloring books. Eventually, after many years of hard work, he got a contract to mass produce religious sculptures and figurines for a television shopping network. The original PMTP chapel was opened in 1985 on acreage near Branson, Missouri, which Mr. Slaughter bought from a group of Mennonite farmers.

Frank Jr. was married and had a wife and eight children. After his tragic death in a skiing accident, his widow and children ran PMTP until 1995, when it was sold to a consortium of Belgian investors. The Belgians tried to stay true to Frank Junior's vision, except that they added a chocolate shop and a store where they sold lace and frilly dresses—all decorated with the distinctive wide-eyed PMTP children.

After watching the film, Ireme and Doray went to the gift shop. As they entered the doorway, they were greeted by a costumed figure. He was a handsome young man with straw-colored hair and fair skin. And the tiny wings were a dead giveaway. He was a Precocious Minutes "Angel" and tour guide.

"Hi! My name is Giles."

Ireme could see that Doray was immediately taken with this mysterious figure.

"Do you want to be my friend?" Giles said.

Doray nodded.

The Angel Giles led them through the magical world of PMTP. At the beginning of the tour was the biggest room in the park, the PM Gift Shop, which had the largest selection of PM figures in the world, including dozens of special figurines that could only be purchased on site. Collectors came from all over the world to buy these limited edition PM figurines.

The variety of figurine designs was enormous, from the American History series to the Bible Tales series. The American History series included a porcelain set of figurines depicting Pocahontas and Capt. John Smith. The face of Pocahontas was a slightly darker shade than John Smith's, but the features were identical—all racial characteristics were melted away—so there was no real difference between Pocahontas, Martha Washington, and Betsy Ross.

Unlike Walt Disney's Pocahontas, it would be hard to imagine this child-like figure running through the woods or picking up bear cubs to kiss them, much less putting her own head under the executioner's axe to save the life of Captain John.

The Bible Tales series figures were drawn with flat features, and the characters were indistinguishable from each other. Of course the figure of Mary was several shades lighter than Pocahontas, and even a couple of shades lighter than Betsy Ross. As in some religions, the skin color tended to reflect a particular shade of theology—in this case Mr. Slaughter's moral theology of pastels and porcelain.

Each of the ceramic figurines was designed to show some patriotic event or inspirational story from the Bible. The violence of history was avoided, and only the G-rated world of smiling and pious figures was shown. In this world David did not slay Goliath, Moses did not strangle the Egyptian overseer, and Jesus did not suffer the crown of thorns, the lash, or the cross. It was a world of all things bright and beautiful, with only nice thoughts and pure notions allowed admittance.

As Giles led the way into the hall, Ireme noticed that Giles had a slight limp. It was a barely noticeable limp, but something about this infirmity bothered Ireme—as if human frailty did not belong in the sweet and pure world of Precocious Minutes

Giles took them to the food court and extolled the virtues of the humble hamburger and the individually packed bags of potato chips. The plates and cups were all Styrofoam and the forks were (Caucasian) flesh-colored plastic. Ireme saw a young woman working at her spot at 7th Heaven Bar-B-Qued Angelic Wings and wondered, "Does this girl see the job as a mere job, or is it spiritual fulfillment?"

Soon, Giles took them into the garden and they walked along, past the flowers, past the ornate iron and brick gates, past the channels and waterways and decorative islands. Just ahead they could see the crown jewel of PMTP, the Angelic Chapel.

Over the years, millions of visitors have come to PMTP to see the Angelic Chapel. As you cross the bridge over the waterway, you can see the great bronze doors and the smiling faces of the PM Angels where they were cast into the metal. The bronze doors have a strange inexplicable beauty to them, which seems a bit out of place among the porcelain figurines, or at least it seems inexplicable until you learn that the doors were cast—at no small expense—by master artisans in Romania. The bronze doors where shipped here and installed in a special PMTP event only last year.

Passing through the doorway, you find yourself in the foyer of the Angelic Chapel. Standing in the small room is a life-size bronze statute of the founder, Frank Slaughter, Jr. The statue depicts his last moments on earth. Mr. Slaughter was wearing skis, and a ski pole was shoved through his chest. This memorial statue was done by Italian master artisans who did the statue in the manner of statues of the ancient martyr, Saint Sebastian. The difference is that, where St.

Sebastian was pierced by arrows, Mr. Slaughter is pierced by a ski pole—and has a rather more surprised look on his face than St. Sebastian.

Ireme tried to divert Doray from the statue, so she quickly pulled him into the Angelic Chapel. Along the walls and across the ceiling there were many pastel-colored murals, each one illustrating a Bible story. The lives of Abraham, Moses, and King David covered the left wall. The New Testament stories of The Nativity, the Three Wise Guys, and the Star of the East filled the right wall. There was no blood or gore. Nothing was seen of the Crucifixion or the Stations of the Cross. Instead the happy stories of the Woman at the Well, Nicodemus up a Tree, the Last Supper, and so on, covered the walls and the ceiling. Their guide, young Angel Giles, took great pains to explain each picture.

The most prominent part of the chapel, the space above the choir, was filled with an enormous mural of Heaven. In this inspired illustration of Heaven, as Giles explained it, the small children standing in line to speak to Jesus are, in fact, the souls of aborted fetuses—the unborn—who are now in Heaven and waiting in line to speak to their Creator. It wasn't clear if they wanted to ask something, or perhaps they were waiting their turn to explain something to Jesus. But Ireme had trouble looking at the mural without feeling some small unquiet emotion deep down inside.

Along the walls leading down from Heaven there were wispy clouds and several other children. According to Giles, the picture of the child in the wheelchair—floating in the clouds—was a representation of a local boy who died of bone cancer in Branson. Another boy was a teenager who died in an auto accident along Highway 65, between Branson and Springfield. The third child, a small girl, died in a house fire nearby.

People could exit the chapel through a hallway on either side. The hallways were also religious exhibits, in this case of Bible stories recorded in stained glass. One of the halls led to a Room of Memories & Remembrance, where there were dozens of large ledgers. Visitors could write the names of loved ones—either children or other family members who had recently passed away. From here the hallway led back around through another hall and out to the front foyer.

From there, young Giles led them through the garden and out to the smaller Victorian Wedding Chapel, where couples could get married and then enjoy their wedding night at one of several Victorian-style cottages located just beyond the RV Park.

Giles reminded them that the food court, the RV Park, and the evening show—the Glory-Full Fountains—were all reasonably priced and open seven days a week, except for Christmas Eve. The evening show included laser light displays, fireworks, and a ride on the Glory Hole Train. There were special discounts for seniors, and all ministers and their families got in free on Tuesday, Wednesday, and Thursday. All bus drivers got a free pass and ate free in the food court seven days a week.

Doray thanked the Angel Giles, and then Ireme and Doray walked across the parking lot to a large, squat building near the road. This was the famous Mrs. Frank Slaughter Personal Museum of Bible Art. Not many people knew it, but just as Salvadore Dali had his wife Gala urging him on in his painting, Mr. Frank Slaughter had Mrs. Frank Slaughter constantly inspiring him to greater and greater heights of religious expression.

This building housed Mrs. Slaughter's private art collection, which she had purchased in Europe and brought here to PMTP for display. The collection included several copies of Biblical paintings by Old Masters, mixed in with dozens of works by local artists. It was generally known as the best collection of Biblical religious art in Missouri, and perhaps even the whole Midwest.

As Ireme and DoRay entered the gallery building, an elderly woman gestured to them from behind a cash register. She said, "Let me mark your tickets for tonight's Glory-Full Fountains Light Show and you can go on in the museum."

Ireme fidgeted with her purse and said, "We don't have tickets for the show."

The lady smiled and said, "Visiting the Mrs. Frank Slaughter Personal Collection is only $5.95 for adults and free for children under twelve."

Ireme opened her purse and searched for the $5.95, but all she had was their bus fare back home, held safe in a white envelope, and about three dollars and change. She dutifully placed the three one-dollar bills on the counter next to the cash register while she searched for enough quarters, dimes and nickels to make up the difference. Meanwhile two young couples came through the door and stood behind her in line.

The woman behind the counter said, "Just forget about the extra change, Dear. You and your son can go over there and join that tour. It just started a few minutes ago and it has only five people in it." The woman picked up the three dollar bills and dropped them in a large jar for donations, placed next to the cash register, and then she shooed Ireme toward the tour group standing in the hallway.

As Ireme and DoRay walked toward the group, she saw that the people in it were all gazing at a huge oil portrait. It was a bluish painting of God's hands in heaven, holding a tiny fetus; and in the background were the bright acrylic blues and dark reds of the universe, with clouds of stars and dozens of planets. The effect of the blues and reds was enhanced by tiny blue glitters that the artist had lovingly placed on the night sky. Near the right hand corner, the blues and reds trailed off into a swirl and then formed an American flag. As Ireme and DoRay joined the group, the tour leader—an elderly woman with light blue hair and a bright pink dress—smiled at Ireme and DoRay. The elderly woman's voice cracked with passion as she struggled to overcome the hoarseness resulting from a long day's service to the Lord, consisting mostly of nonstop talking.

The guide described the symbolism of the painting, which was the crown jewel of the PMTP Private Collection. "Here the blues represent God's love and the reds are the Blood of Jesus, shed on the Cross for all mankind. We can see that the colors flow seamlessly into the reds and blues of the American flag, and the stars of the heavens become the 50 stars of the flag-and God's hands holding the tiny baby . . . well that part should be obvious, because we all know that God is Pro-Life."

The blue-haired lady led the tour group down the hall, passing many wood, glass, plastic, and plaster sculptures, and a special display of dozens of clay figures created just last week by the 5th graders at the God's Harvest School. There was even a face of Jesus, in white-colored pottery, whose eyes followed you as you walked past. As they stopped at each painting, the tour guide pointed out the symbolism. Amazingly, there was a special display of religious cowboy art by a local artist. A large painting of cowboys included three telephone poles, all looking like crosses and symbolizing the Crosses of Calvary. The young cowboy leaned against the middle cross—the cross of Jesus—as he contemplated a glowing red light in the night sky, off in the distance. Nearby another cowboy was reading from his

Bible and witnessing to a third cowboy. The Christian cowboy wore a white hat and rode a white horse, while the other cowboy wore a black hat and rode a black horse. The black cowboy sat with one foot in the flames of the campfire, symbolizing the fires of Hell. Meanwhile the rocks near their feet also carried a message-each stone had either a Bible verse or an image from the New Testament. A large stone with an open hole was the tomb of Christ, left open after his escape from death. Meanwhile, barely visible in the far right-hand corner was a posse of cowboys who had finally caught up with Judas and were lynching him from an olive tree. In the background was a yellow banner, which read, "Mission Accomplished."

Near the door to the next gallery was a crucifixion scene painting—actually it was originally a paint-by-numbers painting. But this one was decorated by a local entomologist who used the wings of hundreds of butterflies & moths to add color. Each wing reflected dozens of rainbow colors, giving the painting a remarkable sheen, even under the hard florescent lights.

Next to this was a long rectangular painting of Jesus on the cross. The blood flowed freely from the wound in his side and poured along the left side of the painting. The blood was filled with tiny images representing soldiers, wars and bloodshe—from the Revolutionary War to the American Civil war, and on. A prominent place was given to the Iraq War, which was (evidently) won by the aircraft carrier Abe Lincoln, in a military action just off of the coast of California.

Meanwhile, on the right side of the painting, the water gushed from the wound in His side, turning into a bright blue ocean. "You can see," she said, "the people who believe in Christ are walking on top of the water, while the atheists and non-believers are drowning in the flood." To people familiar with religious art, the right side of the painting was obviously a careful copy of Gustave Dore's engraving of the Great Deluge, except that it included a brontosaurus and a T-Rex that appeared to be slowly sinking below the waves.

There were numerous copies of the Old Masters in the gallery, and several of these paintings were by the famous painter, Mrs. Otis Swallow of Tulsa, Oklahoma. Mrs. Swallow had made numerous trips to Italy in order to copy these famous religious paintings. Since her death from colon cancer, interest in her works, especially her last paintings, had dramatically increased. Her last works included a self-portrait of Mrs. Swallow with her favorite dog, Tootles, which hung in the lobby of the PMTP food court. Mrs. Swallow was also quite famous for her paintings of Princess Di, Madonna, Mother Teresa, and a painting of President Reagan which still hangs in the National Airport in Washington DC.

The last and most spectacular painting in the collection was a portrait of Jesus on the cross, done life size with bright acrylic paints. The tour guide said, "Last week I was leading a tour and there was a young woman standing under this picture, called 'Our Lord on the Cross.' She was crying. I asked her what was wrong and it turned out that she was deaf. We got an interpreter who told us that she was crying because . . ." Here her voice trailed off and cracked, and tears formed in her own eyes. ". . . Because she saw that Jesus' right hand is making the deaf sign for 'Love' and she saw this and knew it was a message just for her."

Indeed Jesus' left hand, pierced with the iron nail, did seem to form the hand sign for "Love." Meanwhile his left hand seemed to point toward a wispy cloud, off in the background, and sunbeams in the distance. As she looked at the face, Ireme thought of her own home back in Chicago.

Ireme, struggled to hold back the tears, and then she dropped the last of her change into the donations box near the exit.

Ireme and Doray had to run to catch the city bus. Ireme thought about visiting the gift shop one more time and catching a later bus, since they had to pass through it anyway to exit PMTP, but Doray seemed anxious to leave and she just knew she'd find something in the gift shop more important than bus fare. On the way out she thought about visiting the PMTP Antique Barn or the PMTP Bible Bookstore next door, but it was clearly getting late. The city bus was pretty unreliable after 6 p.m. and they couldn't possibly walk all the way home.

The bus finally arrived, and Ireme and Doray climbed aboard. On the way home the bus passed The Shepherd of the Hills Tower. This enormous tower was advertised as the largest erection in Branson, and you could look over the entire valley from its summit. Ireme really wanted to visit there, too, someday. But as it was, she was barely able to make the rent and buy food with her paycheck. She patted Doray's hand and said, "Maybe next month we can visit there . . . I've heard they have Chinese sheep."

TWENTY-ONE

The Wednesday night service arrived and Bobby was ready for it. The camera was set up to record his sermon, and at least half-a-dozen reporters had already shown up to get reactions from the congregation about the mysterious Rapturing of ministers from a church bus between Nasty, Colorado, and Dodge City, Kansas.

Bobby waited near the door for Ramrod Steel to arrive. Bobby had called him earlier, and Ramrod had made a point of mentioning that he was bringing a guest. Ramrod seemed a little mysterious about the guest, but Bobby was too excited to question him. As Bobby watched, their car pulled into the parking lot and Ramrod and a mysterious woman got out and walked up to the church door. Bobby thought there was something vaguely familiar about the woman, but he couldn't quite place it.

Bobby escorted Ramrod to a seat near the front, positioned so that the camera could get a good profile shot of Captain Steel. Bobby had worked all afternoon on his sermon, and he was determined to blow the front row out of their seats.

At 7:00 promptly the choir began to sing "Does Jesus Care?"

Does Je-sus care when I've said Good Bye
To the dear-est on earth to me,
And my sad heart aches Till it near-ly breaks,
Is it ought to Him? Does He care?

O yes, He cares, I know He cares,
His heart is touched with my grief
When the days are wear-y, The long night drear-y,
I know my Sav-ior cares. (He cares)

Bobby signaled the choir to finish the refrain in a muted voice as he picked up his Bible and stepped up to the podium.

Bobby gave a long, involved prayer, ending with "And may God help our friends in Colorado and elsewhere who are missing their husbands and fathers who have gone on to Heaven before them to prepare a place for them. Amen, and Amen."

Then the new Music Director, David Doom, launched into a rousing rendition of "Power in the Blood."

Would you be free from your pass-ion and pride?
There's power in the blood, power in the blood;
Come for a cleans-ing to Cal-var-y's tide;
There's won-der-ful power in the blood.

The choir launched in with the refrain:

There is power, power, won-der work-ing power
In the blood of the Lamb;
There is power, power, won-der work-ing power
In the pre-cious blood of the Lamb.

David the Doominator shot back with the next verse:

Would you be whit-er, much whit-er than snow?
There's power in the blood, power in the blood;
Sin stains are lost in its life-giv-ing flow.
There's won-der-ful power in the blood.

The choir tried to cut him off with the refrain, but David joined in and sang with them.

There is power, power, won-der work-ing power
In the blood of the Lamb;
There is power, power, won-der work-ing power
In the pre-cious blood of the Lamb.

Rev. Bobby dropped his arm and the choir dropped to a light hum, repeating the chorus. He quickly launched into his sermon:

"Brothers and Sisters, here I stand before you. There is a new world beginning here for us today. There is a vast new world to conquer—for Jesus!"

A hail of "Amens" rose from the crowd.

"This afternoon I got down on my knees and I prayed and I prayed. I asked God to tell me what we could do to build His church, to build His Kingdom here on earth."

Rev. Bobby dropped to his knees.

"That's right. I got DOWN on my knees and I prayed and prayed for an answer. And you know what? God gave me His answer. God gave me His message for this church.

"And this is the Real Thing. This is the new world order that God promised us. God spoke to me. God gave me a message. It's a message that He wants us to share WITH THE WHOLE WORLD. It is time for us to send a message of Hope, a message of Salvation. It is time to say 'Wake up world, and hear God's own Truth.'

"Those of you who have been watching the news know what I'm talkin' about."

A murmur of Amens came from the crowd.

"Those of YOU who have been watching the news KNOW what I'm talkin' about!"

A chorus of Amens filled the air. Reverend Bobby smiled and continued.

"In Colorado this morning a whole bus load of ministers was taken up to Heaven. God came down and carried them away, just like he carried away Elijah in his fiery chariot. God saw that these men were His people, and so He took 'em—wham, bam, and they were gone! Up to Heaven.

"God has taken up His people in The Rapture! We know this because God has given us His proof."

Bobby stepped down from the dais and went to stand by Ramrod.

"We know this because God has taken our friend, our beloved pastor, the Reverend Doctor Bill Eous. We know this because God has taken our friend, our sister, Mrs. Ireme Steel. We know that God has taken a lot of people to Heaven, our friends and our family. And some day GOD is gonna take US TOO!

"God told us that The Rapture is STILL GOING ON TODAY. Most educated people think that The Rapture is just a one-time event. They think WHAM! and the whole thing is over and done.

"But that's not true. No, The Rapture is not over. And it doesn't matter what any of the scholars tell you. The Rapture is not over until God's people say it's over! Say HALLELUJAH! And Amen."

The crowd responded with loud "Hallelujah" and several loud Amens trailed in at the end.

"Yes, Brothers and Sisters, Hallelujah and praise God. The miracle of The Rapture is happening right now, as I speak to you. Across the world thousands of Christians are being taken up into Heaven. They are being carried away by God's angels, just like those ministers in Colorado. True believers in Jesus, our Lord and Savior, are being carried UP TO GOD!

"And you, all of you sitting here today. You still have a chance to be carried up to Heaven, just like Brother Bill, just like Ireme Steel, just like little Doray Steel. Yes, you have a chance to escape the Torments of Hellfire. You CAN be saved!

"You ask me, Brother Bobby, 'What can I do to be saved?'

"And I say to you, 'You must preach the gospel, you must preach the Good News.' Amen!

"You must spread The Word. You must tell all mankind that the New Rapture is upon us! God's angels are a comin' down and carrying away God's people. You have one last chance to escape the trials and torments of The Great Tribulation.

"It was preached by Saint John in his book of Revelations. You all know that the Four Horsemen of the Apocalypse are coming, and the Seven Seas are gonna spill open, and Death, and Pestilence, and Disease are going to destroy this world. But even though the world will suffer under the iron heel of The Antichrist, some of God's people WILL survive. They will escape this terrible suffering and join their loved ones in Heaven.

"So what will happen to us? What will happen when we finally reach Heaven?"

Rev. Bobby grabbed his black leather Bible from the podium and swept down to the front of the stage, waving the book and pointing to the sky.

"It says in the book of Revelations 7:9: 'After this I beheld, and lo a great multitude, which no man could number, of all nations, and kindred, and people, and tongues, stood before the throne, and before the Lamb, clothed with white robes, and palms in their hands; And they cried with a loud voice, saying, 'Salvation to our God which sitteth upon the throne and unto the Lamb.'

"And all the angels stood around the throne, and around the Elders and the four beasts, and fell before the throne on their faces, and worshipped God, Saying, 'Amen: Blessing, and glory, and wisdom, and thanksgiving, and honor, and power, and might, be unto God for ever and ever. Amen.'

"And one of the Elders answered, saying unto me, 'What are these who are arrayed in white robes? and whence came they?'

"And I said unto him, 'Sir, thou knowest.'

"And he said unto me, 'These are they which came out of great Tribulation, and have washed their robes, and made them white in the blood of the Lamb. Therefore are they before the throne of God, and serve him day and night in His temple; they shall hunger no more, neither thirst any more; neither shall the sun burn them. For the Lamb which is in the midst of the throne shall feed them, and shall lead them unto living fountains of waters; and God shall wipe away the tears from their eyes.'"

Bobby stopped and nodded his head.

"This is God's promise to us, that when we reach Heaven, we will be rewarded by serving Him day in an' day out, forever and ever in His holy temple, 24/7. And we shall wear white robes washed in the blood of Jesus."

There was a murmur of Amens from the congregation.

"In Heaven we shall ALL wear white robes washed in His blood!"

The crowd was visibly stirred by the sincerity and emotion in his voice. A loud chorus of Amens chimed in. Then Rev. Bobby cued the choir, and they began singing in a muted voice "The Kingdom is Coming."

From all the dark plac-es Of earth's heathen rac-es,
Oh see how the thick shad-ows fly!
The voice of sal-va-tion A-wakes ev-'ry na-tion,
Come o-ver and help us, they cry.

The sun-light is glanc-ing, O'er ar-mies ad-vanc-ing
To con-quer the king-doms of sin;
Our Lord shall possess them, His presence shall bless them,
His beau-ty shall en-ter them in.

Bobby held his arms over his head, as the choir dropped to a light hum. He yelled "Praise God" and then stepped down from the platform and went directly over to stand near Ramrod Steel (and his strange lady friend). Bobby smiled and put his hand on Ramrod's shoulder.

"Friends, brothers and sisters, you need to find peace with The Lord, the same way Brother Ramrod did last Sunday night. I'll be waiting here for you, right here. Come on up. Dedicate your life to Christ. It's time to come Home. Don't you know where your home is? It's time. It's time to come home."

Dozens of people got up from their seats, ready to come forward, ready to dedicate their lives to Christ.

"You need to help others, but first you need to help yourself."

The people streamed forward as the choir started to sing softly, "Help somebody today" with its refrain of "Help some-bod-y to-day, Some-bod-y a-long life's way; Let sorrow be ended, the friendless befriended, Oh, help somebody to-day."

The people moved forward down the aisles, slowly, as the music carried them forward.

Rev. Bobby wailed, "It's time for YOU to help someone!"

And that someone was Bobby Black.

After the service Bobby shook hands and greeted the dozens of people who had come forward that night to dedicate their lives to Christ. Bobby made a point of talking to the strange woman, who turned out to be Missy Duncan, a lady friend of Ramrod's. And there was still something vaguely familiar about her, but Bobby couldn't put his finger on it.

"Boy, he doesn't let much dust gather on his wife's pillow," Bobby muttered as he closed the front doors and locked them. Then he went directly to the camera and pushed the button to open it. He was slightly surprised to see a tape rather than a DVD-RW. "Hmmm, we need to get a new camera," he thought to himself. He popped out the tape. "Anyway, this little gem is going to the duplicating service first thing in the morning."

* * *

Mark Doody labored all night over his story on Nickelay Dubyah the Younger. It was a difficult task. There was no way, given what he knew, that Mark could write a fluff piece. So he decided to go with his instincts, and he wrote a scathing article about how the Secret Police had imprisoned a group of protestors, how they had detained and tortured at least a dozen leaders of the Full Moon Party, and the fact that Nickelay Dubyah had ties to several unsavory characters, including Jonathan Seagull and Todd Fox-Halburton. Mark also suggested that Seagull and Fox-Halburton had probably conspired to fabricate evidence against Iraq, suggesting that Iraq had access to nuclear materials and technology.

Mark sent the story to *Weekly Whirled News*and then headed for the airport. "No point hanging around here!" he thought. But he didn't plan on the fact that the airport had been closed, according to a flyer taped to the front door, "due to the terrorist attack on Nickelay Dubyah, our future Fearless Leader."

Mark scrambled to find another way out of the country. His story was already printed in the evening edition and broadcast on the WWN network news. Then the story was picked up by the Arabic news channel, All Jizz Frah, and by television stations all over the world. Of course, only two or three radio stations and one independent television station in Texrectumstan carried the story. But this story was too big to ignore, and eventually even the Half Moon Party's television network was vaguely hinting at the story while simultaneously attacking it, as part of their "fair and balanced" news policy.

Mark went to the coffee bar across from his hotel, hoping to hide from the Death Squads he was sure were now looking for him.

Sitting in the back of the bar was Dick the Welshman, his moustache half off and the vein in his temple doing a pizzicato of hosanna from the caffeine overload.

"You've got to help me get out of the country!" Mark whispered as he grabbed Dick by the arm.

"Why?"

"Why? Because I wrote a story criticizing Dubyah. He's sure to have me killed."

"No. Don't worry about it. You're perfectly safe."

"Don't you understand? I criticized Dubyah! My life isn't worth two cents."

"No, seriously, don't worry. Even a vicious thug like Dubyah knows enough not to kill a reporter. At least not so soon after the story came out."

"Really? That's a relief. I guess."

"I'd say you have at least two or three weeks before he sends a hit man to kill you."

"That *really* makes me feel better."

Dick stirreded his coffee around with a spoon, then examined the edges of the spoon where the silver plate had been eaten away.

"So, Mark, why did you do it?"

"Hey, it was your idea to expose Dubyah and his cronies."

"I guess so. But why didn't you say anything about the bio-weapons lab in Africa?"

"I included the bio-weapons lab in my story, but they didn't print it."

"Ah, that explains it."

"Explains what?"

"Tell me, Mark, after all these years of working in the media, how is it you still don't have the slightest idea of why some stories are published and others aren't?"

"Uuuuuh, I don't know."

"Just for an example, why do you think those small radio and television stations in Texrectumstan reported a story that was critical of Dubyah? They could have just ignored it."

"I don't know. I guess they believe in Freedom of the Press."

"Haaa! That's a good one, mate. Freedom of the Press, I'll have to remember that one."

"Well, then why did they carry the story?"

"It's really very simple. The media hate a lopsided election. Every time a politician gets out too far ahead of the opposition, the media moguls decide that they have to go after him and try to damage him."

"Why?"

"A television station makes money by selling adverts. If an election looks like a cakewalk, then neither side buys much advertising. The guy who's ahead doesn't need to, and the guy who's losing can't afford to buy any. So the reporters attack the guy who's ahead, hoping to make the election more even. If the election gets close, then both sides buy a lot of advertising. In this case the story isn't going to hurt Dubyah much anyway, but a lot of his stooges who are standing for election in marginal districts will have to buy more advertising."

"So why didn't the television stations run the story on the bio-weapons lab? That might really change the election."

"True, it might. But if it didn't, and Dubyah still wins, then you have to deal with a powerful enemy who can cause you a lot of trouble. The bio-weapons story is like a vial of anthrax: you have a devastating weapon on your hands, but if you use it, you might get the stuff all over you, too."

"So, no one will run the bio-weapons story."

"No, they'll run stories on minor corruption, cheating on your wife, telling off-color jokes in public, picking your nose, and that kind of thing. That's how they got Howard Dean. And you remember the American politician who got slammed for calling someone a 'Makaka.' The politician was ahead in the polls, and that's why he got hit for using a racial slur. But these reporters never do a serious story—especially about genocide—not unless they're sure they can destroy the guy with the first shot. And even then, Dubyah has a lot of close friends in the world of corporate media. Why would they want to hurt him politically? He's their boy."

TWENTY-TWO

Big Al now faced the greatest challenge of his career. A journalist for one of the country's largest cable news channels wanted him to appear as a guest on her talk show Thursday morning. He was going to have to face tough questions, not just from a professional journalist, but also from an audience full of nonbelievers who would tear his story of The Rapture to shreds.

Big Al called his accountant, Andy Arthur, and asked him to transfer all his cash to offshore banks—just in case he had to make a run for it.

He could see the headlines: "Massive Fraud in Church Pedophile Case," "Elder Smith Resigns in Conspiracy Case" and "Elder Allyson Evades Arrest—Last Seen in Haiti."

All these worries rushed though Big Al's brain, causing his thoughts to collide in a train wreck of emotions. In the end, Big Al went to the television station and sat in a chair quietly as they did his makeup. In those last quiet moments before going on stage, Al decided he had to tough it out. He said to himself, "I've bluffed my way through worse than this! I've done it before, and I can do it again."

The television studio in Chicago broadcast Big Al's image by satellite to the headquarters of the cable news channel. The show's host was Ms. Coulter Aho-Waxxer, a popular TV celebrity who had recently married her agent. Coulter chatted with the audience while waiting for the program to start. Normally, the show would be taped in advance, but Elder Allyson was a last minute replacement for a controversial rap star who had been arrested for possession—he claimed to have been "possessed" by a demon when he attacked a police officer.

Being part of a live broadcast made Big Al even more nervous. It only got worse when Big Al saw a teenage boy in the audience wearing a T-shirt that said, "My pastor got Raptured in Nasty, Colorado, and all I got was his lousy T-shirt."

Coulter began:

"Today on Good Morning This Week we meet Elder Allyson Smith. Elder Smith was on the bus two days ago in Nasty, Colorado. That was the day over forty ministers vanished into thin air, as witnessed by Elder Smith and the bus driver. Many people believe that this is only the latest case of people being carried up in The Rapture. As most of you know, according to some Christian religious beliefs, The Rapture marks the beginning of the Tribulation—a period of time when The Antichrist will rule the earth."

She turned to the monitor and Big Al appeared on screen.

"Tell me, Elder Smith, in your own words what happened that day in Nasty, Colorado."

"Actually, Coulter, it was between Nasty and Lamar, Colorado."

"Sure, go on."

"We were driving down the highway and I turned to talk to one of the ministers—I believe it was Reverend Bierce—and as I spoke to him, he slowly vanished. He just dissolved in mid air."

"That's fantastic. And what happened then?"

"I looked around, and the other ministers were slowly disappearing, too. They faded away into empty air. All that was left was their clothes. So the bus driver and I drove on to Lamar and tried to report what happened to the authorities."

"So you talked to the police?"

"Yes, but they had never heard of such a thing before."

"And what did you do?"

"While we were standing near the empty bus, someone said that it might have happened because of The Rapture."

"Can you explain for our audience what The Rapture is?"

"According to the Bible, at the beginning of the End Times, all of God's Chosen will disappear. They will all be taken up to Heaven in The Rapture. Those of us who are not taken to Heaven with have to endure a period of time called The Tribulation. During this seven-year period, The Antichrist will rule the earth. And at the end of seven years, Christ will return. He will destroy The Antichrist, and Jesus Christ will set up His Kingdom on earth."

"Interesting. So the disappearance of these ministers fits with the prediction of what will happen when the world comes to an end."

"Yes, there are several predictions in the book of Revelations which speak of the coming Tribulation. Many scholars believe that the Rapture will signal the beginning of these Last Days."

"And do you believe that this is what happened?"

For a second Big Al felt his gonads itch. Should he lend this story the authority of his office as a High Elder of the church? Or should he let The Rapture just hang there as one possible explanation of the mysterious vanishings? Big Al decided to push the envelope and proclaim a miracle: The Rapture did it.

"Actually, Coulter, I am sure. With each passing day, I am becoming more and more convinced that these holy men were taken to Heaven."

There was a murmur from the crowd. Big Al wasn't sure if they were agreeing or not.

"Let's see what our audience thinks."

A portable microphone was handed to an elderly woman sitting near the back. With the microphone pressed to her face, the woman said, "I believe that God has taken these ministers to Heaven."

Several other audience members agreed with this idea.

Then another person said, "Maybe they were abducted by aliens."

Coulter said, "Well, let's bring in our next guest, Mr. Dug Adams. Mr. Adams was the victim of three alien abduction attempts, and he is here today to share with us his terrible ordeal."

The camera cut to a distraught looking young man. He was wearing a baseball cap covered with aluminum foil.

"Mr. Adams, thanks for coming. Can you tell us what happened to you?"

"Yes, Coulter. It was like this. I was taken on board an alien spacecraft, and I was anally probed about three dozen times before I managed to escape. It was a horrible, terrifying experience. It was so dreadful that I feel myself drawn back to the woods where I was originally abducted. I can't stop myself."

"But why would you go back there?"

"It is important, as part of the healing process, to validate your experience. At least that's what my therapist says."

"Aren't you afraid that the aliens might abduct you again?"

"I'm ready for them this time," Dug said as he reached into his pocket and pulled out a small bottle. "Now I always carry a bottle of Astral-Lube."

The camera moved in for a close-up shot of the bottle covered with a stars-and-smiling-full-moon logo. Dug continued, "The Astral-Lube Company has generously offered to make me their new spokesperson."

After a brief commercial, selling feminine hygiene products, radial tires, and a 30-second spot for the amazing new product, Astral-Lube, the show continued.

Coulter was back on camera, and she said:

"In our first segment, we heard Elder Allyson Smith describe for us the miracle of The Rapture, where over forty ministers were taken by God and carried to Heaven. They were actually taken from a moving bus! Then we heard Mr. Dug Adams describe his horrifying ordeal at the hands of alien abductors."

The camera panned over the audience, who were all smiling and doing high fives.

"Well, let's go to our next guest, Brother Anil Roberts of Miami. Brother Anil, tell us about your experience."

"First I want to say Hi to all my cousins in Miami, Oklahoma," Brother Anil said, smiling and waving. "Hi cousins, hi Ma!"

"Okay, Brother Anil, now why don't you describe for us what happened that night, the night when your father disappeared."

"Sure, my Pa and me were out fishin' on Grand Lake. We were in our aluminum boat, the one with the new fish detector, but we weren't catchin' much. It was gettin' dark, so I said to Pa, I said, 'let's go on home' and he was of a mind t' go, too. But before we could pull in the cinder block an' chain, this big cloud came down outta the sky and two men appeared—poof!—right there in front of us. And what was really weird was they was standin' on the water. They walked across the lake and came right up to us. They didn't even step into the boat. They just stood there on the water, smiling at us."

"What happened then?"

"They was dressed in white robes and they had long white beards. The older-lookin' one said his name was Herman and the younger one was Thurman. They said they's called 'The Witnesses' and they have come to earth to serve mankind."

"Wow! That's fantastic."

"Sure is. The younger one, Thurman, he saw we had a cooler in the boat. And he says, 'you have any wine in there?' and I says no, but I have a couple of beers. And so I gave him a bottle and showed him how to screw off the top. I'll be, if he didn't chug the beer, right there, and then toss the bottle into the boat."

"That's really fantastic!"

"I'll say! Then he said, 'You wouldn't believe how long it's been since I've had a cold one,' or somethin' like that, and he smiled and waved his hand over my head and said, 'bless you, son' and then both of the men disappeared into the air."

"What do you think he meant when he said, 'bless you'?"

"I don't know. But ever since then that the rash I had on my privates has cleared up and my ex-wife came back to me and my old houn'dog likes me again."

"Fantastic! And what happened then."

"Well, my Pa was taken up in the cloud, along with the two Witnesses, and we didn't see him again for three days. He just show'd up at the door one night. But Pa says he cain't remember what happened while he waz gone. But I'll tell you this. He lookt like he waz rode hard and put away wet!"

"Thanks, Anil, that's a truly fantastic story."

Coulter moved out into the audience and held the microphone out to a young woman who said, "So why did the two men appear on the lake? Why did they choose you?"

"Any ideas, Anil?" Coulter said.

"Well, they must a had a reason for comin' there. So Pa and me decided to start our own church overlookin' the lake. It's called The Two Witnesses Community Church of Grand Lake, Oklahoma. Last week we poured the foundation, and the walls should come by truck from the factory in Missouri next week. My brother is gonna run the business end of the church. He has his GED and he's even takin' classes at the A&M college."

Coulter smiled and said, "Last question."

A guest in the middle aisle asked, "How white were their clothes? I mean, were they cotton, or wool, or some kind of polyester, or something?"

Brother Anil thought about this one for a few seconds, then said, "Well, I guess they was pretty white. I mean we all know that in Heaven the robes are washed in Jesus' blood, so I guess they must be white as snow!"

The audience began smiling and talking. The camera shifted back to Coulter.

"So, everyone, thanks for joining us today. It's really been a fantastic experience for all of us. And I hope I'll see you again tomorrow!" Coulter smiled and waved as the cameras flashed to the different guests: Elder Allyson Smith, Dug Adams, and finally Brother Anil Roberts.

Big Al was greatly relieved. After the show, hel went up to Coulter and thanked her for having him as a guest.

"It really was a lot more pleasant than I expected."

"We were only too glad to have you," she said. "After all, this kind of audience participation is powerful, cutting edge stuff. It's an important part of 21st-century television journalism."

Big Al was puzzled. "What do you mean?"

Coulter smiled and said, "All you have to do these days is to remember to say 'fantastic!' instead of 'bullshit!'"

* * *

Thursday morning Reverend Bobby rolled over in bed and used the remote to turn on the small television. It was an interview show, and Big Al was a guest. Bobby watched the television intently. He was glad to see Big Al throw his ecclesiastical support behind The Rapture. It made his own job a lot easier.

Bobby still wasn't sure why Big Al had staged the disappearance of the ministers in Colorado. It just didn't make sense. Unless there was some reason he wanted them to disappear.

Bobby climbed out of bed, doing his best to avoid waking Dee and Ann. They both looked pretty well worn out from last night's romp.

Bobby decided that he was going to have to learn how to pace himself—that mix of cocaine and Viagra was powerful stuff. Bobby turned off the small television and walked to the kitchenette where his clothes were hanging on the back of a kitchen chair.

Most people in this same situation would think seriously about taking a shower before going to work. But Bobby enjoyed the smell—the mix of sex and alcohol and sweat. It was simply not in his nature to do things differently or to concern himself with what the people who now worked for him might suspect.

Bobby had a chance to think on his way to the church. He used his cell phone and called his new Office Manager, while driving through the morning rush hour traffic.

"Take the tape off my desk and send it to the duplication service. I want to be able to sell copies of last night's sermon on our web site as soon as possible. Tell them to rush it . . . and make sure to bill the duplication costs to New Rapture Church."

In the back of his mind Bobby knew there was something he was forgetting, but he just couldn't bring it to mind.

TWENTY-THREE

Mark decided to follow Dick the Welshman's advice and go back to his hotel. It would be better for him to act normally. No point angering Dubyah by acting as if something was wrong. The best way to handle it was to bluff his way through.

And Dick might be right. Thursday morning, after breakfast, one of Dubyah's personal envoys appeared at the hotel and asked Mark to accompany him. Mark's first impulse was to leap screaming from the balcony.

But that would have been the coward's way out. Besides, the windows were shatterproof and sealed from the outside. So Mark gathered up his tape recorder and his note pad. And he followed Dubyah's envoy down to the street, where two thugs loaded Mark—a bit roughly—into a waiting limo.

Things started to look bad. They looked especially bad when the limo pulled up to the front gate of the largest prison in the city. The State Prison, called Abu Ghrabas, also served as headquarters for Dubyah's Secret Police. The prison was legendary for the perverse tortures that took place there.

The envoy noticed the look of horror on Mark's face.

"Do not worry," he said, in perfect English, "Nickelay Dubyah and his brother, Jebbulah, are making an announcement at the prison today. Dubyah simply wants you to witness the event and write about it."

"But what kind of announcement would he make at a prison?"

"Last week Dubyah promised some kind of amnesty to the condemned. I believe he plans to free some political prisoners, as a sign of his generosity and good will."

Mark looked around and said, "What happened to all the protestors who were here yesterday?"

The envoy smiled, benignly, and said, "They were moved this morning to the Official Protest Area."

A chill went up Mark's spine as the thought about the men and women who were probably, at that very moment, being unloaded at the old nuclear power plant. Mark had seen the effects of radiation poisoning up close while visiting Chernobyl, the site of a nuclear accident years earlier. The memory of diseased flesh and deformed children was hard to forget, even for someone like Mark, who had seen first hand the horrible effects of war.

For a brief moment Mark remembered Dick the Welshman's warnings. And Lucy Washington's prediction. Could Nickelay Dubyah be The Antichrist? It seemed hard to believe.

The envoy led Mark to an auditorium, where over a hundred naked prisoners were seated in metal chairs. Most wore chains, usually leg irons, and a few wore primitive-looking handcuffs, too. Several had been beaten—recently—and Mark saw the dried blood on their faces and the bruises. One of the prisoners appeared to be coughing up blood.

Mark and the envoy sat in chairs that overlooked the auditorium. As Mark took out his tape recorder, he saw Dubyah the Younger and his brother Jebbulah walk out onto the stage. "I will translate for you," the envoy said. He placed his hand on Mark's arm and took the tape recorder. As Jebbulah spoke, the envoy translated:

"Prisoners! You have the great honor today of enjoying a visit from Nickelay Dubyah the Younger, soon to be the Fearless Leader of Texrectumstan."

The guards prodded the prisoners on the edge of the crowd with their bayonets, and the prisoners began to cheer loudly.

"My brother has given a great deal of thought to your situation. He feels deeply for you. You are all prisoners, guilty of crimes against the state. But you are not beyond redemption. My brother has thought and thought. He has prayed to Allah for His Truth. And Allah the Merciful has given us an answer.

"Throughout the Middle East and Europe there is turmoil. In Palestine the Jews and the Palestinians are at war. In Eastern Europe the Christians fight with Islam. All this fighting is an offense in the eyes of Allah. And this fighting must end. It is the will of Allah.

"The differences that separate the Christian from the Moslem, and the Moslem from the Jew—these differences must be ended. Dubyah the Great and Merciful has discovered a solution to these differences:

"First, the Christians and Jews must accept that Mohammed is a true prophet of Jehovah.

"Second, all Moslems must accept that the prophet Jesus was more than a mere prophet, that he was greater than Mohammed and a true Messiah.

"Third, the Jews and Moslems must accept that Jesus was the Messiah foretold in prophecy and that the Messiah will return someday to bless Israel.

"All these things must be accepted as Truth. On that day, the three great religions can be joined together as one—Moslem, Jew, and Christian—with the promise that Allah, or Jehovah, will bless this land and establish the reign of peace forever and ever.

"This is the roadmap to peace that our Fearless Leader has given us. And now it is time to discover whether you will enjoy the blessings of peace, too."

The prisoners shifted uneasily in their chairs. Mark could smell the odor of desperation in the room. What did Dubyah want?

Jebbulah continued. "Today you will be offered the chance to leave this place. Your Fearless Leader has decided, in his infinite wisdom, that any man who, today, chooses to accept Jesus the Christ as his savior will be set free."

There was an angry murmur in the crowd. The guards quickly moved in with their bayonets to quell the noise.

"Let me say this again. Moslem, Christian and Jew must join together. We must come together as one. We must be all of one religion, one faith, one God. All of you, today, have the opportunity to be the first to join this movement. Any man here today who asks forgiveness of his sins and accepts Jesus the Christ will be given his true freedom.

"Any man who refuses will be beaten and returned to his cell."

There were voices in the crowd. One prisoner stood, in the midst of the rest and called out with a strong voice:

"Praise Jesus! I am saved!"

Another prisoner struggled to his feet and called out:

"Yes, Jebbulah, I am saved, too! Praise Jesus the Messiah!"

Others stood and cried, "Me, too, I love Jesus, I love Mohammed, I love even the damned Jews. I will be saved, too."

"Praise Dubyah! Praise Jebbulah! I, too, wish to praise Jesus with all my heart."

Another prisoner rose and called out, "Bless you, mighty one, I will praise the name of Jesus. I will worship him all my days. I will love him as one greater than Mohammed, and much greater than the Jewish prophets."

The proclamations of love for Jesus, and the thanks, went on for several minutes. Finally Jebbulah raised his hand for silence.

"Then all of you are free men!"

The room practically exploded as dozens of naked men who had lost everything suddenly found themselves the possessors of new hope. The prisoners began hugging each other, smiling and laughing.

"But first," Jebbulah said, "we must have a baptism. Each of you who has accepted Jesus as the Messiah must be washed in water."

The prisoners, most of whom had not bathed in months, or even years, welcomed the idea of cleanliness. They cheered, "Yes, yes! Let us bathe in the water."

"Since we have no water tanks for baptism," Jebbulah said, "we will have to send you through the showers."

The guards moved forward and began herding the prisoners through a large door. The door led through a passageway to where showers had been hastily erected. The large doors closed behind them.

Left behind was a lone woman prisoner. She sat in a metal chair off to the side and behind a curtain, where she couldn't be seen by the male prisoners.

"Who is she?" Mark said.

"The woman? She killed her husband, after he beat her. He raped their daughter, then beat her when she complained."

By that time Dubyah had noticed her sitting there, too. Several of his advisors began arguing. The envoy said, "They cannot send her to the shower. She must be kept separate from the men."

Dubyah gestured for her to come forward. The woman hesitated, then stood. Dubyah spoke and the envoy interpreted:

"Dubyah says, 'Do you accept Jesus as your Savior?'"

The woman, covering her face as best she could, nodded assent.

"He says, 'Get down on your knees and beg forgiveness from your God.'"

The woman kneeled before Dubyah and Jebbulah, then she said some words in so low a voice that she could barely be heard.

Dubyah drew his .45 from his holster, put it to her head and pulled the trigger.

Chunks of skull and brain matter flew in all directions. Jebbulah, who was standing nearby, was splattered with her blood.

Jebbulah began shrieking in anger.

"Jesus!" Mark said. "He blew her brains out! There's blood all over his brother's clothes."

The envoy smiled a tight, grim smile, "No, Jebbulah is angry because he wanted to do it."

As the envoy led Mark from the room, he could hear yells, screams, and choking sounds coming from some place just down the hall, and then, gradually, quiet.

The prisoners had been genuinely surprised by what came out of the showerheads.

* * *

Repeated phone calls to the police had gotten Cloye nowhere. The Chicago cops were not very interested in finding her mother and brother. She had called all of her mother's family and friends—some of them twice. But none of them had any idea where Ireme could have gone. And all of Ireme's church friends were convinced that Ireme and Doray were now residing comfortably in Heaven. No matter how Cloye pressed them, her mother's church friends kept insisting that Cloye accept that her mother was now "in a better place." Cloye was physically and mentally exhausted from dealing with her mother's friends, and especially their cheery certainty that Ireme and Doray were now in Heaven. Cloye was especially bothered by Missy's claim that Ireme and Doray were enjoying dinners of manna and roast lamb, washed down with Christ's blood.

That evening Cloye went to church with her father and with his new lady friend, Missy. The service made her nervous. She just couldn't believe that The Rapture had taken her mother and brother. At the same time she felt an indefinable and uncertain need to believe Reverend Bobby. He seemed so earnest, so caring. It was hard to keep her skepticism focused, especially in the face of his determined faith, not to mention the loud response of the congregation.

When they got home, Cloye was surprised—at least a little—when Ramrod said that Missy was going home. Then Ramrod offered to drive Missy home, and his motivations became clearer. "Good grief," Cloye said, as Ramrod smiled and led Missy out to his car.

This gave Cloye a chance to think. Had her mother and brother been carried away to Heaven? Her brain told her no. But her emotions said yes.

Wasn't it better to imagine her mother and brother safe in Heaven? They, at least, wouldn't have to face the trials of the coming Tribulation.

If there really was such a thing as a Tribulation. Or was that just another boogey-man story told to keep people in line?

Is that what it was all about, control?

TWENTY-FOUR

On Friday morning Ramrod got a phone call from Hadshe Dunhim. Ramrod rolled over and picked up the princess phone. He found it a little unsettling to talk into the face of a Precocious Minutes angel. Two years ago Ireme had bought the phone and insisted Cloye put it in her bedroom. Cloye had refused, and so she lost both the phone and the phone line.

So the phone was put in the master bedroom, instead. And Ramrod had to use it.

"Ramrod, is that you?"

"Hadshe? What time is it?"

"It's nine in the morning. Don't you have a flight today?"

"I think so, maybe sometime this afternoon."

"Well I know. I'm on the same flight."

"You are?"

"Yes," there was a hesitation in Hadshe's voice, "Is that a problem?"

"No, it's not a problem. I look forward to seeing you."

"You do? I was waiting for you to call. And now I'm starting to wonder. You haven't even tried to see me since Sunday, and here it is Friday. I mean, it's not like you have a wife at home and have to sneak around." There was a short pause. "She is still gone, right?"

"Yes, Ireme is gone. And I've been spending a lot of time at church."

"Church? Ireme's church?"

"Yeah, sure. Where else?"

"I was beginning to get jealous. I was thinking that maybe you have another woman in your life."

For a second Ramrod thought about confessing that he had gone out with Missy several times. He had even taken her to his wife's church. But why would he deliberately hurt Hadshe's feelings that way?

"No, no," he said, "Why would you think that?"

"It's just that you used to seem so . . . eager, to move on with your life."

"No, it's just that I have to go by the church today, before the flight."

"Okay. So I'll see you later?"

"Yeah, for sure."

Ramrod hung up the phone and lay back on the bed. His head was shrouded in the clouds of a Precocious Minutes pillowcase. It was truly a dilemma. Here he was with two women after him. On the one hand, Hadshe was a stunningly beautiful honey blonde. She could easily work as a supermodel, or maybe she could have a few years ago. But, on the other hand, he also had Missy, who was strikingly good looking, too, but in a more enigmatic way. Maybe it was the platinum blonde look. For some reason the Mona Lisa painting came to mind—probably because Ramrod had just seen the painting on the front cover of Cloye's art textbook.

No matter what happened next, Ramrod knew he was going to feel guilty about it later. This was the story of his life. It had been—how many years was it? He couldn't remember how long it had been since he and Ireme were really completely happy. But Ireme was gone. And now these two amazingly beautiful women were—for some reason Ramrod couldn't quite figure out—seriously pursuing him, almost competing over him. Ramrod had always believed in happy endings. Now, in spite of all the sadness—the loss of his wife and his son—his life was going to have a Happy Ending. It was just like Brother John said at the service last night, in his homily: "Life is Like a Chinese Massage."

Ramrod got dressed, went downstairs and said goodbye to Cloye. Some vague idea still rolled around in the back of his head. Why was Cloye at home instead of at college? Ramrod decided to ask Ireme when she got home, but then he realized that Ireme was gone, forever, and for the first time in his life he—Ramrod—was going to have to deal with this problem, whatever it was, all by himself.

He drove over to the church and saw Reverend Bobby there, walking toward the front door.

"How's it going, Captain Steel?" Bobby said.

"Fine, fine. I think you wanted me to come by here today."

Bobby couldn't quite remember what it was he wanted to talk to Ramrod about, beyond encouraging him to come to church on Sunday. But as they came through the door, Bobby saw a stack of boxes sitting in his office and realized that these were the DVDs and tapes from his Wednesday service. The box had been opened, and a tape was on his desk.

Bobby handed it to Ramrod.

"I was wondering if you would watch this tape and give me your reaction?"

Ramrod took the tape and flipped it over. There were no labels on the box.

"What is it?"

"Oh, it's just my Wednesday night service. I think you might be able to give me a few pointers on how I can improve the way I speak. Maybe Cloye could watch it too. It might be just what she needs to start believing—to join the side of the angels."

Bobby slapped Ramrod on the back and pointed him toward the door. Moments later, as Ramrod drove away, Bobby still had that irritating feeling that there was something important that he had forgotten.

Ramrod drove directly home with the tape. As he walked inside, he could hear Cloye upstairs. He knew that she was putting Ireme's clothes into bags and moving the bags into Doray's bedroom. Ramrod couldn't face the sight, so he called to Cloye.

"Honey, could you come downstairs for a second?"

Cloye was dressed in blue jeans and a t-shirt. Her hair was tied with a bandana.

"Cloye, I have to leave for the Atlanta flight today. I just wanted to say 'I love you' before I left. And I want to ask you to do something for me."

"What do you want me to do?"

"Reverend Bobby gave me this tape. He wanted you to watch it. He hoped it would convince you about the thing, The Rapture thing, and maybe you would want to join your mother's church. It's our church now, too."

Maybe this tape would have the answers that Cloye needed to finally make a commitment to Christ. Ramrod was sure that it would only take a small effort to bring Cloye over to "the side of the

Angels." He pressed the tape into Cloye's hands and kissed her on the forehead. Then he grabbed his briefcase and left.

While driving to the airport, Ramrod closed his eyes (briefly) and prayed that Cloye would come to understand Jesus, once and for all.

* * *

Cloye sat in her room. She had already cleaned the house and washed her father's clothes. His uniforms had been sent to the laundry. The house was still a mess. Cloye thought about trying to box up the rest of her mother's personal things and put them in storage in the attic, but she just couldn't bring herself to do it. It would be easy enough to leave Doray's room as it was. It could be a little shrine to him.

Wherever they were, Cloye hoped that they would come home soon. She began to wonder about going back to college. How would her father be able to get along without having her around to clean up after him? Then she realized that, by January, her father would almost certainly have a new wife. It was clear that Ramrod intended to get on with his life, and sooner rather than later.

She went downstairs and put the tape in the machine and turned on the television. She sat watching the Wednesday night service, listened to the hymns, heard Reverend Bobby preach on The Rapture and saw Bobby put his hand on Ramrod's shoulder, as if to comfort him in his time of loss.

Wouldn't it be easier, she thought to herself, to simply accept that her mother and brother were gone, taken to Heaven by Jesus? Wouldn't it be right to think of them in Heaven? Wouldn't it be wonderful if they were happy and healthy and living in perfect Peace and Joy in another world, a world without cares and suffering?

Cloye got down on her knees in front of the television and began to pray, perhaps for the first time in her life.

"God. Wherever Mom and Doray are, I hope they are with you. Or I hope that, at least, you are looking out for them if they're not in Heaven. And look out after Dad, too. He needs your help, maybe even more than the rest of us."

Cloye's eyes and heart followed the closing of the service. She saw the dozens of people coming forward, walking toward the altar and accepting Jesus as their own Personal Savior. And what about

Cloye? She was tempted, deeply tempted to pray for Forgiveness of her Sins (such as they were), and pray for Salvation and pray for Jesus to give her his Love. She could love Jesus just like these people did. And Jesus would love her back. And she knew that Jesus would love her, too, because . . . well, because. And then she couldn't think. How would she know if Jesus loved her?

People in the church were always talking about how they loved Jesus. And they claimed that Jesus loved them back. But most of these people were still deeply troubled. It seems like loving Jesus just gave them more stuff to worry about. Like, am I really saved? Do I love Jesus enough? Does Jesus really love me?

And these worries were piled on top of the worries they already struggled with every day. Wasn't life hard enough without having to deal with a lot of stuff that was all vague and mysterious and supernatural? What is God's love? How do you know you have it?

Cloye remembered that day, years ago, when she walked into the bedroom and saw her mother wrapping a Christmas gift and putting a card on it that said:

[From: Santa]

Cloye had confronted her mother. With a sad, questioning timbre in her voice she looked at her mother and said, "Does this mean there is no Santa Claus?"

Her mother nodded.

"Does this mean there is no Easter Bunny . . . and no Tooth Fairy?"

Again, her mother nodded.

"Does this mean there is no God?"

Ireme's face flushed, "Of course there is a God! Whatever gave you that idea? Of course there is a God, and he is everywhere and he is watching you right now!"

"Just like Santa's elves?"

"Go to your room, young lady!" Ireme shrieked.

That was the first time Cloye had challenged Ireme's faith in God. And, with each day that passed, they could never again go back to the way it was before, when they both innocently believed.

Cloye watched the service close, and then she saw it.

At the end of the service, the tape changed to something else. It took a few seconds for her mind to recognize the action she saw on the TV screen for what it was. It was some kind of amateur porn! And there was the Reverend . . . doing *what?* . . . Oh my God!!!

Cloye was stunned. And she knew, suddenly, that the whole New Rapture was a pious fraud, just like the Easter Bunny, just like Saint Nick.

And just like God.

The Rapture was a fraud.

Ireme and Doray were gone. Somewhere. They were making a new life for themselves away from Ramrod and herself. Ireme had left Cloye behind. She chose raising Doray over being a wife to Ramrod and a mother to Cloye. But maybe it would all turn out for the best. Maybe, while she was out there on the road, her mother would learn something about life.

And Cloye, too, had to get on with her life. She didn't even bother to shut off the tape. She went to the garage and got into her old Buick, drove to the public library, and logged on to the Internet. She found the website for the state university in DeKalb and printed the application forms for getting admitted for the Spring semester.

* * *

Rev. Bobby didn't quite understand the panic in her voice when he got the call.

"The videos! They have . . . they have . . . something on them!"

It was Mary's voice. And there was something wrong with the new videos.

"Calm down, Mary. What's wrong with the videos?"

"There's something on the them at the end. It looks like a homemade porn video! I shut it off after two seconds. But it was enough."

In took all of four seconds, but the chain of events quickly assembled in his mind. The video of Dee, Ann, and himself . . . he had taken it from their camera and then? Bobby had taken the tape to the church and put it in his desk, on top of a few blank tapes and DVD-RWs. And then? Could they have picked up *that* tape and sent it to the duplicating service by mistake? It would have almost two full hours of Bobby, Dee and Ann naked, frolicking, and fornicating in their apartment! But no, Mary had said the material was at the end of the video.

Then the sickening truth hit him. Brother Ervil, who operated the church's video equipment, must have asked Mary for a blank tape before the service; and she had gone to his desk and pulled out the tape of him, Ann and Dee. Ervil had recorded over that tape—and the service was only an hour and a half long!

And he had given a copy of the tape to Ramrod Steel!

"Call Brother John and tell him to meet me at church! Now!"

Bobby got on his cell phone and called David.

"You've got to meet me at the church, right now!"

"I am at the church," David said.

"Get Captain Steel's home address from the membership directory. Then meet me in the parking lot. I'll be there in five minutes."

* * *

Brother John Doyle was in his room at the YMCA, trying to sleep off a bottle of "Thunder Chicken." He heard a knock on his door, and it sounded like the Russian army marching through Poland. With aches and pains shooting through his body, John lurched forward and opened the door. It was one of the Y's desk clerks.

"What?"

"You have an urgent message from the church. They need you over there right now. It sounds like an emergency."

Brother John closed the door and slowly pulled on his cowboy boots. He found a half-empty bottle of cough syrup on the floor next to yesterday's underwear and decided to finish the bottle before trying to stand up.

After sitting on the bed for a few minutes, John felt his head stop swimming. He pulled on his clothes, stood, and left the room, wondering if he could find his car.

* * *

Reverend Bobby pulled into the parking lot, where David was standing. Bobby hated to have to draw David into something like this, but he had no other choice. If worse came to worst, he would use David as the fall guy. After all, could David explain how his fingerprints had gotten into Ramrod Steel's house? Who would the cops believe? A three-hundred-pound rapper or a distinguished minister and servant of the Lord?

David climbed into the passenger seat, and a few minutes later Brother John arrived. John looked a bit shaky, as if he was coming off a bender. His hands were trembling and he looked pale and sick. Bobby decided that, hey, as long as he didn't get sick in the car, they'd be okay.

"So what's so important?" John said.

"I accidentally gave a tape to Captain Steel. We have to get it back, before he looks at it."

"What's on the tape," David said.

"You don't want to know."

Bobby shifted the car into gear and they headed to Ramrod's house.

It was a quick drive, and no one spoke. Bobby parked on the street in front of the Steel house. The front door was locked, but with a little encouragement David was able to press against the door and the frame until the door popped open. All three men began a search of the house. There was no tape to be found.

Bobby and John were in the living room when they heard the garage door start to open. They looked out the window and saw Cloye driving into the garage.

"Well," John said, "Do you want me to do her?"

"No, let's get out of here."

They found David in the kitchen, looking for the tape in the refrigerator. All three went out the patio door and then around the house to their car. As they drove away, David reached into his pants and pulled out a tape.

"Oh. Here's the tape you were looking for. It was in the VCR. Imagine that."

"Do you think anyone watched it?" Bobby said, a note of fear in his voice.

"There's no way to know. It was at the beginning, but somebody might have rewound it."

TWENTY-FIVE

As they left the prison, Mark decided to risk asking Dubyah's envoy about the execution he had just witnessed. He was still in shock, wondering why Dubyah would want him to see such a thing. Mark suspected that it was some kind of subtle threat, like "This could happen to you, too!"

Mark said, "There is something that I want to ask."

"Ah, you are probably wondering about the execution. I was wondering how long it would take you to say something."

"I guess I don't understand. Why did they execute that poor woman?"

"You saw that she accepted the prophet, the Messiah, Jesus, as her Savior?"

"Yes."

"And she is now a saved one, as you say."

"Yes, once she accepted Jesus as her Personal Savior, then she became one of His people."

"And when she dies?"

"She goes to Heaven."

"Yes, she goes to Heaven. So where is she now?"

"Well, she must be in Heaven—or on her way there."

"Very true, so you see, the Great and All-Powerful Nickelay Dubyah, soon to be the Great and Exalted Fearless Leader of Texrectumstan. He has done her this great favor."

"Favor? What favor?"

"If she had lived on, she might . . . how do you say it? . . . back-slide. But now she is dead and she is in Heaven with her new Lord and Master, Jesus the Christ."

"Oh."

"And better. Because she dies in fullness of her belief, Allah the Great and Merciful will accept her into Heaven as a blessed martyr."

"I don't understand."

"She will get to wear the white burkah washed in the blood of Jesus."

Mark thought about this for a few minutes. It seemed to make sense to him, in a bizarre sort of way. Wasn't it better to send her directly to Heaven, rather than take the chance that she might sin again and fall away from the purity of her belief? It was just like a "Get out of Hell free" card.

"I guess you're right," Mark said.

"And not only that. As a martyr to Allah she also gets to have seventy-two virgins—seventy-two boy virgins."

As they rode along in the car, Mark visualized seventy-two hunky young men, tanned and well oiled. These hunky young hunks gathered around her—serving her wine, popping olives in her mouth, and peeling their bananas.

"This is all part of the New World Order," the envoy declared, as he smiled.

Suddenly the vision of the seventy-two male virgins faded, and all that Mark could bring to mind was the image of the professional wrestler, Val Venus, standing in the middle of a wrestling ring and pulling off his towel as he smirked and said, "Helloooo, laaadies!"

* * *

At the same moment, Bobby Black, David the Doominator and Brother John were driving back to the church, as Bobby gripped the stolen video in his clutches.

Ramrod Steel was arriving at the airport, wondering if he was going to see Hadshe, and how much of Hadshe he was going to see during the flight to Atlanta and back.

Ireme Steel was standing behind the counter at 7th Heaven in the PMTP food court and wondering if she should try to home school Doray.

Cloye was filling out an application for the university in DeKalb.

Lucy was traveling, third class, on a slow boat to Africa where she planned to join the Sisters of Joy in Jesus and do charity work among the poor and starving masses.

And Mark Doody was being escorted into the presence of the Nickelay Dubyahs, *Pere & Fils*, as today they planned the ceremonial transfer of family authority from the father to the son.

* * *

During the ride from the prison, Mark had several minutes to think about what he had seen. Dubyah and Jebbulah had promised freedom to a room full of prisoners and then executed them without mercy, and without any concern about innocence or guilt. They had even pulled the trigger on the woman themselves. What could it all mean? Did Dubyah really believe that he could establish One World Religion? Did he think he could parlay control over his small country into dominance over the old Soviet Union, and then the world? What would the New World Order mean for Christians? What would it mean for the Jews? What would it mean for Moslems?

Even more important: What would it mean for Mark?

Dubyah's envoy led Mark into the Grand Reception Hall of the Main Palace. This hall, with its row upon row of marbleized columns, was built as a replica of the original Hall of Kings that was the Wonder of the Ancient World a thousand years ago in Iraq. Nickelay's Grandfather, "Double Dutch" Dubyah, had ordered it built many years ago to celebrate his own coronation.

Nickelay's father, Nickelay the Elder, was already there, dressed in his gold crown and his ermine robes, resplendent in scarlet silk—all embossed with the famous image: The Tiger of Texrectumstan.

Mark was escorted to a place near the back, but a spot with a good view of the proceedings.

Then, Nickelay Dubyah the Younger entered the room and swaggered gracelessly across to the imperial throne. His father kissed him on both cheeks and then made his pronouncement:

Little Dubyah was to become invested with the leadership of the Dubyah clan, upon his making "The Gesture of Fealty" to his illustrious father.

Once Little Dubyah had abased himself in the observance of this ritual, he would be the undisputed master over not only the adoring citizens of Texrectumstan, but over his own family.

Little Dubyah got down on his knees, as his aged father stood, turned, dropped his pants, and bent over.

Mark could see, there on his left buttock, a tattoo of a tiger. And right next to the tiger appeared some vague markings—which looked to Mark like a tattoo portrait of Judge Bork.

Mark pulled the envoy's sleeve and said, "What is that next to the tiger?"

"That is a portrait of the grandfather, Ascott Werrin Dubyah the Third. He was the founder of the dynasty. He made the family fortune by selling oil to the Nazis."

Mark heard a shushing sound.

A grim looking official stared at Mark and then put his finger to his lips, suggesting that Mark be quiet during the ceremony. He followed this by dragging his index finger across his throat, in an ancient gesture that translates as "long life to those who remain quiet."

They watched as the elder Nickelay backed toward Dubyah, his wrinkled and flabby butt cheeks wagging. The old man yelled out:

"Kiss my left behind!"

Young Dubyah skoogied forward on his knees and planted a big, juicy one on his elder's wrinkled buttock. The old man laughed and jiggled, forcing Dubyah to get a little more than he'd bargained for.

Jebbulah Dubyah stepped forward and proclaimed:

"All hail the new ruler of Texrectumstan!"

This announcement was hailed by cheers and whistles. Nickelay Dubyah was now the undisputed ruler of his clan. And, by extension, he was now ruler of Texrectumstan, too.

TWENTY-SIX

Ramrod Steel sat in the airport lounge and emptied his briefcase onto the small table before him. He sat and stared at a pile of bills, part of a stack of mail that had accumulated over several days. Ramrod had brought the mail with him to the airport so he could sort through the bills while waiting for his flight. He was doing a kind of triage to see if he had to deal with anything really important. Now, as a single father, he had to do better with his time management. Ireme was no longer here to do it for him. He reached for the mail.

There were the usual offers of credit cards, a discount card from a local video store, a card for 10% off any purchase of hair care products at JC Penney's, a sheet of coupons for the local pizza joint. Ramrod shuffled through the pile, tossing most of it in the trashcan next to his table.

An oversized glossy letter caught his eye. It was embossed with a gold seal and had words printed in what looked like ornate Hebrew letters. It was one of *those* letters, the kind that he wouldn't have looked at twice only a few weeks ago. The return address said: The Jesus Family Human Genome Project. And it gave a street address in Dayton, Tennessee.

On the back of the envelope it said: "We chose to build our genetic testing laboratory here in the same town where the famous Scopes Monkey Trial took place back in 1925. We chose this place, over any other town in the US, because this place will see the final triumph of Science and Christianity—working together for the greater glory of Our Lord Jesus. And you can help!"

Ramrod opened it. The letter had a yellow post-it note attached that said: "Dear Brothers and Sisters in Christ, won't you take a moment to find out if you are part of Jesus' real human family?"

A bit confused, Ramrod opened the letter and found a picture of an olive tree, with the names of people stuck to various limbs—Joseph, Mary, Jesus Christ, Mary Magdalene, Baby Jose, James the brother of Jesus . . . The letter included a newspaper clipping which described the recent discovery of the Jesus Family Tomb in a small suburb of Jerusalem. Individual stone boxes for burying bones, called ossuaries, had been found for each member of Jesus' Family. They included his wife, Mary, and his son, little Baby Jose. And it also included his brother James and several other brothers that Ramrod had never heard of. According to the letter, Jesus Christ had three more sisters, all named Mary too.

As he thought about it, Ramrod remembered the TV special that Ireme had talked about only a few days before she disappeared. Ireme said that archeologists had found the tomb of Jesus and his family in Jerusalem. Genetic testing of dust from the stone boxes had shown a family relationship. She even had the copy of *Newsweek* with the picture on the cover of the stone box taken from tomb.

The letter went on to describe how the Jesus Family Genome Project was doing genetic testing of people from all over the world.

They were locating people who were blood relations, and perhaps even descendants, of Jesus Christ and his family.

A return address card said: "You might already be a part of Jesus' holy family!"And "Are you ready to claim your blessing?"

The letter went on to describe a woman living in Edinburgh, Scotland who had discovered—thanks to the Jesus Family Human Genome Project—that she was a direct descendant of Jesus' younger sister, Mary II. Shortly after this, the lady had received a healing of her pancreatic cancer.

An elderly gentleman, living in a nursing home in Portland, Oregon, had discovered that he was descended from Jesus' cousin, John the Baptist. After making this amazing discovery, the gentleman had won the Euro Internet Lottery and was now living in a mansion in Scottsdale, Arizona.

Another woman had discovered that she was descended, by way of her Great Grandfather, from the brother of Jesus—a man called James the Just. After making this wonderful discovery she had invested all her money in a German pharmaceutical company and made a fortune, only six months later, when the company patented a new set of tests for genetic markers.

A rabbi in Chicago had sent in a blood sample to the Jesus Family Human Genome Project and discovered that he was descended from Moses, Aaron, and a family of the High Priests of Israel. In less than a month, the rabbi inherited a collection of valuable Torahs from his uncle. The eighteen scrolls were worth over $4,000 each.

A Catholic priest in Akron, Ohio, had sent in his blood and discovered that he was descended from the wife of the wealthy Egyptian Lord, Potiphar. A few weeks later he became Bishop of a major city in Ohio

Ramrod read though page after page of glowing testimonials.

All these people had given a tiny blood sample to the Jesus Family Human Genome Project. And all of them had discovered a long lost (and unsuspected) connection to family members who had lived in ancient Israel. And each of them had their life blessed with health, wealth, and happiness—fulfilled in the knowledge that they were now truly a part of Bible history.

Ramrod carefully examined the return address card. Taped to the thin cardboard was a straight pin. The card suggested that he stick the pin in his finger, draw a small drop of blood, and wipe the blood on a small spot on the card-marked with an (X).

Ramrod held his thumb steady as he plunged the steel pin into his flesh. A red ball of blood slowly formed, and Ramrod carefully rubbed the blood onto the (X).

At the bottom of the card it said that *all* blood samples would be tested, and if a connection to the family of Jesus (or some other Biblical figure) was discovered, the person would be contacted by the technicians from the Jesus Family Human Genome Project laboratory in Dayton, Tennessee, and additional follow-up genetic testing would be done. Special attention (and speedy processing) would be given to any blood submitted by a member of the Project's "Honorary Advisory Council." Becoming a member required only a contribution of $200. The letter stated that "Capt. Ramrod Steel" had already been pre-approved for possible membership on the Council. It only required his blood sample and a check to start the process.

Ramrod stuck the card in the return envelope, reached into his briefcase, and pulled out his leather checkbook. He had seen Ireme do this dozens of times, but this was his first experience writing out a check to one of her Christian organizations. It felt good to finally be part of the family.

THE END?

If you enjoyed this book,
check out our web site

www.seesharppress.com